CRYSTALS • GEMSTONES • METALS

In the past few years the value and worth of crystals have dramatically increased. This is due in no small part to the recent discovery by many people that crystals can be used for a variety of *spiritual and magical* purposes.

Modern science has shown that crystals are of great value, and everything from telecommunications to watches makes use of them. The main spiritual use of crystals is as a psychic energy generator and director. The energies thus raised and directed are most commonly used for healing and psychic grounding.

But what is little known is that *crystals, gemstones and metals have their own inherent powers and abilities just waiting to be used!* The secrets of these powers have been hidden in rare and unusual books. In the following pages Scott Cunningham reveals these secrets along with the results of his own personal research in order to present the most comprehensive book on the magical properties of crystals, gems and metals ever.

MAGIC YOU CAN DO TODAY

The magical uses described here do not require long rituals or expensive paraphernalia. Rather, they tap into the innate power of crystals, gemstones and metals! You will learn which can help improve your love life, which can help you study better, which can help improve your financial situation, and which can help you overcome a broken heart.

All it takes is a few stones or crystals or metals, some of which you may have right now! This is natural magic at its finest, with information on over 100 magical items. If you want to make positive changes in your life but don't like the idea of doing complicated rituals, *this is the book for you!* Here is a complete course in natural magic—magic you can use today; magic which has been used for thousands of years.

Whether you study at home or go outside to work, whether you go to school or teach school, whether you are a magician, a Wiccan, or have never even thought of doing magic, the information in this book can help change your life—it may even help save your life.

Now is the time, no matter your age, your financial situation or your health. This is the book that will help you make the changes in your life you want and need. You won't need long periods of study, you won't need expensive tools. All you need to improve your life and the lives of those around you is **Cunningham's Encyclopedia of Crystal, Gem & Metal Magic.**

About the Author

Scott Cunningham practiced elemental magic for over twenty years. He was the author of more than thirty books, both fiction and non-fiction, sixteen of them published by Llewellyn Publications. Scott's books reflect a broad range of interests within the New Age sphere, where he was highly regarded. He passed from this life on March 28, 1993, after a long illness.

To Write to the Publisher

If you would like more information about this book, please write to the publisher in care of Llewellyn Worldwide, and we will forward your request. The publisher appreciates hearing from you and learning of your enjoyment of this book and how it has helped you. Llewellyn Worldwide cannot guarantee that every letter can be answered, but all will be reviewed. Please write to:

Llewellyn Publications
c/o Llewellyn Worldwide
P.O. Box 64383-126, St. Paul, MN 55164-0383, U.S.A.

Please enclose a self-addressed, stamped envelope for reply, or $1.00 to cover costs.
If outside the U.S.A., enclose international postal reply coupon.

Free Catalog from Llewellyn

For more than 90 years Llewellyn has brought its readers knowledge in the fields of metaphysics and human potential. Learn about the newest books in spiritual guidance, natural healing, astrology, occult philosophy and more. Enjoy book reviews, new age articles, a calendar of events, plus current advertised products and services. To get your free copy of *Llewellyn's New Worlds of Mind and Spirit*, send your name and address to:

Llewellyn's New Worlds of Mind and Spirit
P.O. Box 64383-126, St. Paul, MN 55164-0383, U.S.A.

Other Books by Scott Cunningham:

Magical Herbalism
Earth Power
Cunningham's Encyclopedia of Magical Herbs
The Magical Household (with David Harrington)
Wicca: A Guide for the Solitary Practioner
The Truth About Witchcraft Today
The Complete Book of Incense, Oils and Brews
Magical Aromatherapy: The Power of Scent
The Magic in Food
Earth, Air, Fire and Water: More Techniques of Natural Magic
Living Wicca
Spell Crafts: Creating Magical Objects
          (with David Harrington)

Video:

Herb Magic

Forthcoming:

Traditional Hawaiian Religion & Magic

Cunningham's Encyclopedia of Crystal, Gem & Metal Magic

by
Scott Cunningham

1994
Llewellyn Publications
St. Paul, Minnesota 55164-0383, U.S.A.

FIRST EDITION, 1988
Thirteenth Printing, 1994

Cover photo by Bob Bretell
Inside photos by Frank Schneider
Book design by Terry Buske

Library of Congress Cataloging-in-Publication Data
Cunningham, Scott, 1956-1993
    Cunningham's encyclopedia of crystal, gem and metal magic.

    (Llewellyn's sourcebook series)
    Bibliography: p.
    Includes index.
    1. Amulets—Dictionaries and encyclopedias.
2. Talismans—Dictionaries and encyclopedias. I. Title.
II. Title: Encyclopedia of crystal, gem and metal magic.
III. Series.
GR600.C86   1987   133.4′4   87-46256
ISBN 0-87542-126-1

Llewellyn Publications
A Division of Llewellyn Worldwide, Ltd.
P.O. 64383, St. Paul, MN 55164-0383

*This book is dedicated to
Robert Thompson,
who introduced me to
tourmaline, rockhounding
and the pleasures of
crystals and stones*

Acknowledgments

To John Burchard, who shared quartz crystal information with me years ago; to Charmoon for his magical and spiritual insights; to the nameless rockhounds and dealers who have (often unwittingly) expanded my knowledge of stones and their magical uses; to Leon of Isis Bookstore in Denver for his assistance; to deTraci Regula, Ed, and Marilee for loaning rare books; and finally to the Earth, our home, for providing us with these beautiful, powerful tools. May we collect and use them gently and with love.

Credits

Special thanks go to these people for their services and for providing the rock specimens necessary for the completion of this book: Muriel Deneen, Terry Buske, Julie Feingold, Phyllis Galde, Berg's Rockhound's Paradise (Prescott, Wisconsin), and Brett Bravo.

CONTENTS

Introduction

Crystals, stones, metals. Amethyst for peace. Quartz for power. Silver for psychism.

From the earliest prehistoric times to our technological age we have found beauty, power and mystery within stones. Just as herbs possess energies, so too do stones and metals. With their powers we can change ourselves and our lives.

Stone magic is as old as time. It began when the earliest humans sensed some force or power trapped within the stones that surrounded them. Stones were probably first used as amulets—objects worn to deflect negativity or "evil." Later they were revered as deities, offered as sacrifices, and buried for blessings and fertility of the land. Their use is intimately connected with religion, ritual and magic.

Stone magic has been forgotten by many millions of people today. The Industrial Revolution and two devastating wars destroyed the insular village life in which the old magic was passed from generation to generation.

Today a new awareness of the magical value of stones and metals has swept over us. This sudden interest is unprecedented in history, and, like the growing use of herbs in magic, is another manifestation that people are finding their micro-chip lives unsatisfying. Something—*magic*—is missing.

In my sixteen-year journey into the world of shamanism and magic I've become convinced that, at one time or another, every aspect of human existence was governed by magic. Over the centuries we've lost most of this wisdom, but tantalizing fragments remain.

Persons with no interest in magic may think that wearing birthstones is lucky, that pearls are said to bring a bride tears, and that the

Hope diamond is cursed. They may not know why they think such things, but they do.

If we look into the past, to an age where the mystic properties of stones and metals were unquestioned, we find answers.

Stones, like colors, plants and other natural objects, are magical tools which we can use to cause needed change. Transformation is the essence of magic, and stones help us achieve this by lending their powers and providing focal points for our own energies.

After centuries of repressive religious structures and deadening materialism, many of us are awakening to the fact that we have become estranged from the Earth. Executives toss brilliantly hued gems onto black velvet, studying their patterns for hints of the future. Secretaries place moonstone and azurite between their brows to strengthen psychic awareness. Students wear quartz crystal to improve their study habits. The old ways are once again accessible to all who desire to use them.

Stones and metals are keys which we can use to unlock our potential as human beings. They expand our consciousness, enhance our lives, calm our stresses and infuse our dreams with healing energies.

Skeptics say it's in our minds. Magicians say yes, that's part of it. It's also in the stones, in our ritual use of these treasures and in our connections with the Earth.

Stone magic works. It is effective. That's all anyone needs to know to try it out.

In using stone magic we don't turn our backs on technology. I'm not about to give up electricity and the other benefits of our age.

No. We use this old magic to improve our hectic lives, to give us deeper understanding and control over them. It attunes us with the powers which created stones, ourselves, the Earth and the universe, thereby adding the missing ingredient to our often sterile lives.

When a stone lying in a dry riverbed calls you to pick it up, when a shimmering crystal seems to pull your hand, when a faceted jewel set in a ring captures your imagination, you've felt the old powers of stones.

The stones, the magic is waiting. The rest is up to you.

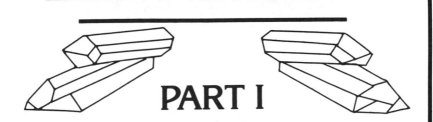

PART I

BEGINNINGS
AND MAGIC

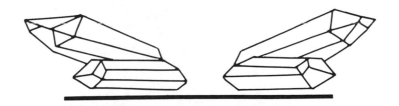

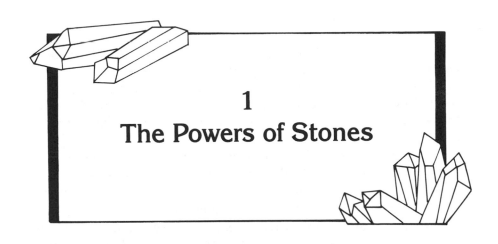

1
The Powers of Stones

Moonlight. A woman stands in her garden. The wind lifts her white scarf into the air as the silver light rains down upon her. In her upraised hands lies a six-sided crystal. She gazes at the shimmering stone, sensing its erratic, disturbing vibrations.

As the breeze dies, it silences a stand of ancient pines that encircle the figure. The Moon seems to glow brighter, and the woman feels its soothing light radiating down from the sky.

The stone calms. Its bizarre vibrations diminish and then grow strong, uniting to form a single, regular pulsation of energy.

As the woman holds the stone higher, its power spills down into her arms, flowing through her like a series of pleasant electric shocks. She grows vibrant and powerful.

After an unmeasureable time, the figure lowers the stone and impulsively touches it to her brow.

Her work is done. The crystal is purified and ready for magic.

Stones may lie deep within the earth or exposed to the Sun and stars. They are dull or prismatic, dense or coarse. Blue, green, red and colors no rainbow dares to display are common among them. Plentiful agate and costly emerald. Transparent, tri-colored tourmalines and opaque marble. Royal purple sugilite and clear quartz crystal.

Stones are gifts of the Earth. They are manifestations of the

1

universal forces—of 'Deity', 'Goddess', 'God', 'Fate'—which created all that is, all that was, and all that has potential of being.

The Earth is one tiny part of a vast energy network. Though once created by it, our planet now contains its own vibrations. Some of these powers, and their manifestations, are shaded and formed to be beneficial to us.

Stones are magical batteries which contain and concentrate the Earth's energies. Many are thought to also be affected by, or at least symbolic of, the planets and luminaries of our solar system. Others have long been associated with far distant stars.

Magic and stones are anciently related. Rocks shaped into animal forms by wind and rain have been used as symbols and as the focus of rites for longer than has been recorded. For ten thousand years, shimmering gemstones have been carried or worn for protection against the unknown. Stones which were scarce, strangely shaped, or that exhibited electrical or magnetic properties are long-time magical tools.

In the earliest ages, stones were carved into images which seem to be religious or magical in nature. They also provided building materials. Tools fashioned from them cut grain, shaped garments, extracted thorns and performed surgery. Stone weapons guarded and ended life. Rocks were heated to boil water eons before the invention of fireproof vessels. Stones were at once beautiful and utilitarian, sacred and profane.

Through the ages, humans have relied on stones to ensure conception, ease childbirth, guard personal safety and health, and to protect the dead. More recently, stones have been used in magic for internal or external change. Moonstones were worn to promote psychic awareness. The amethyst calmed tempers. Peridot was carried to attract wealth. Rose quartz drew love.

Today, five thousand years of stone magic is at our fingertips. Many people are discovering the powers within stones. Working with rocks, these people, stone (natural) magicians, are transforming their lives.

What is this stone magic anyway? How can a few rocks scratched out of the dirt have any affect on anything? Why are quartz crystals, of all things in our technological age, outselling video cassette recorders?

Stones, like herbs, colors, metals, numbers and sounds, aren't inert. They may sit quietly in the earth for millions of years, or rest on a shelf where we placed them last week, but they are active, powerful tools possessing energies which can and do affect our world.

Stones are gifts from the Earth which we can use to improve our lives, our relationships and ourselves. Many are readily available and inexpensive, while others can be gently collected from the ground itself.

Stone magic is built upon simple ideas and has direct results. Using a stone in magic brings its influences and energies into play. *Directing those energies is the magic.*

If you have decided to attune and work with stones, welcome to the world of crystalline magic. You might never leave it.

What secrets lie within the water-worn pebble lying on the beach? What hidden energies pulse inside the stone on your finger, the gems around your neck? Could the very rocks you walk upon draw a love into your life, or help you financially?

Find the answers for yourself. The powers within stones are available to all. Use the Earth's treasures wisely, and they'll bless you with all that you truly need.

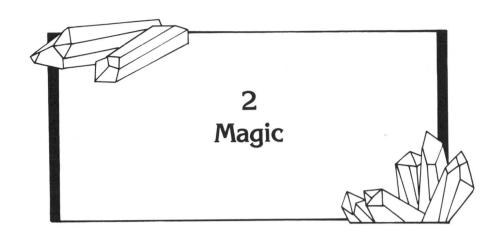

2
Magic

Magic is transformation.
Transformation is magic.
All magic is change; all change is magic.

Stones, crystals and metals, as well as colors, scents, forms, movement, Earth, Air, Water, Fire, insects, animals, ourselves, our planet and our universe, contain energy. It is this energy which permits us to practice magic.

In the philosophy of the magician, the Wise Woman, the shaman, the Kahuna and the High Priestess, this energy descends from the primal, original source. This has been termed 'Goddess', 'God', 'Supreme Deity', 'Fate' and many other names. Countless faiths have created complex ritual calendars and stories concerning this energy. It is that which is revered within all religions.

But this energy source is actually beyond religion, beyond theory or explanation. *It simply is*—everywhere, within ourselves and our planet.

Magical practitioners are those who have learned of this energy. They arouse, release and direct energy.

Contrary to what you may have heard, *magic is a natural process*. It is not the stuff of demons and unsavory creatures, and no 'fallen archangel' lends us the ability to practice magic. These are the ideas of a religious philosophy which abhors individualism. Magic is, in a sense, true individualism, for it allows us as individuals to take control of our lives and work to improve them.

Is magic "supernatural?"

No. The supernatural doesn't exist.

Think about it for a moment. *Super*, meaning extra, outside of, differing from, and *natural*. Outside of nature? Different from nature?

No way! Magic is as natural as stone, as real as our breath, as potent as the Sun.

Stone magic, the use of the energies within stones to effect needed changes, is a perfect example of the naturalness of magic, for what could be more organic than rocks?

Most books written on crystals and stones today are primarily concerned with spiritual development and healing. Few of these works deal with any other aspects of magic.

That's where this book is different. Magic lives on every page. Developing psychic awareness, drawing love and friendship, releasing sexual dysfunction, attracting money and health, sharpening mental powers, inducing peace and happiness—these are the wonders that can be created through the powers of stones.

Magic isn't worked by controlling or dominating nature; again this is a nonmagician's view, another holdover from the "magic is supernatural" idea. In magic we work in harmony with these forces. Magic practiced any other way is limiting and is often merely a strong ego-boost for the magician.

This chapter discusses some basics of magic, in order to make Part II of this book useable. Where 'visualization' or 'directing the power' or 'setting up a stone altar' is called for, you'll know the basics.

But again, as I stress in all my books, I (naturally) write about what has worked for me and what feels comfortable. If my rites and symbols and mental processes don't speak to you, investigate and find the ones that do.

Remember: nature is the teacher. Nature is a phenomenon of magic; it is an illustration in the universal spellbook. If these written words mean little to you, listen to the stones, to the wind, to Fire and Water. Listen and learn.

THREE NECESSITIES

As I first outlined in *Earth Power*, there are three things which must exist for successful magic. These are:

The Need

A need must exist. Usually this is a need which can't be satisfied through other means. Attracting love, guarding your home, obtaining housing or other material objects are prime examples.

A wish for a relationship, or a desire for a new home aren't needs. A need is an empty space in your life or a critical condition (such as ill-health or danger) which must be worked on immediately.

Magic fills that vacuum or corrects the condition, thereby fulfilling the need.

The Emotion

Along with the need there must be emotion. *Emotion is power.* "Seeing red" is an example of this—the face grows hot, the heartbeat increases. These are manifestations of power.

If you aren't emotionally involved in your need, you will be unable to raise sufficient power from any source and direct it to your need. In other words, your magic won't work. If you need to pass an upcoming exam, for example, but you don't really want to, any magic done to improve your chances will fail.

The *emotion* sets the power free to bring the *need* into manifestation.

The Knowledge

This is the way of magic—the techniques which we use to arouse energy within ourselves or natural objects, such as stones, and send it forth toward the magical need.

The 'knowledge' includes visualization, basics of ritual, concentration and the reality of power.

This chapter contains some beginnings of the knowledge.

If we have the *need* and the *emotion* but not the knowledge of how to utilize these things, we would be like a Neanderthal human contemplating a can opener or a computer. We wouldn't know how to use the tools.

Once the need, the emotion and the knowledge are present, we can begin to practice magic.

MAGICAL MORALITY

We practice magic to improve our lives and those of our friends and loved ones. Magic is performed out of love, not hate. It is harmony with nature, not domination.

Many people become interested in magic because they think it's a great way to get rid of their enemies. They see magic as a weapon of anger, rather than a tool of love.

Power is neutral. Electricity, one manifestation of the power, can be used during laser surgery to save life, or to energize an electric chair to end it.

Energy is the same. Our intentions and needs determine its effects on the outside world.

Magic isn't (or shouldn't be) an instrument of selfishness, domination, pain, fear, manipulation, ego-gratification or control. On the contrary, it is life-affirming, infused with love, joy, contentment, pleasure and growth.

As I've said, if I was ever truly hateful of someone (which has never happened), I'd probably throw a punch their way, rather than a spell.

Some people disagree with me on this point and have said so to my face in classes and workshops. I just shake my head, for there's no talking to folks like that. Soon they drop out of sight and are never heard from again.

If you stick your finger into a hot light socket, you get shocked. Practice manipulative magic, you get worse.

The choice, quite simply, is yours.

YOU OR THEM?

It's best to work magic to cause changes within yourself or your life before helping others. In this way, you'll quickly learn how it works and how best to perform it.

This isn't selfishness. Your life is your magical laboratory. Once the experiments have worked, you can apply them to others. Who would trust a magician whose life is in disarray, who is in debt, constantly sick, or emotionally unstable?

VISUALIZATION

You can practice visualization. Close your eyes and see your best friend's face, or your favorite piece of clothing.

Understand? Visualization is simply 'seeing' without the eyes.

Magical (or creative) visualization is forming similar pictures of your magical need. In other words, we 'see' what has yet to be. In a sense, this visualization is the key which moves the energy toward the goal. Forming and perfecting magical visualizations is easy with practice.

If you wish to bring a love into your life, hold a rose quartz and visualize yourself as being involved in that relationship. Even though you can't see the person's face (remember: Magic is not manipulative), see yourself happily with that person. Let the *emotion* of your need, as well as your need itself, wrap you in its warm embrace; then, 'see' the energy from within you streaming into the stone and then out to do its work.

That's magical visualization.

CHARGING STONES

Before using them in magic, stones should be 'charged' or 'programmed' with energy. This is done simply by holding the stone in your projective hand (usually the right, but the left for lefties), visualizing your magical need, and pouring energy out from your body into the stone.

This energy is personal power. It resides within all of us. We can move this energy from our bodies out into stones, candles, metals and other objects to help us achieve our magical goals. The movement of this or other forms of natural energy is at the heart of magic.

See the power flowing out from your body, through your projective hand and into the stone. Charge it with the energy of your magical need—love, money, power, health.

When you know that the stone is vibrating with your personal power, the charging is complete. This simple process, performed before each ritual, will greatly enhance the effects of your stone magic.

THE STONE ALTAR

If you wish, perform your magic—at least, that which is done indoors—at a 'stone altar'. This isn't a place where we worship rocks, of course, but an area set aside for the practice of magic.

Ideally, fashion an altar by placing a large slab of marble or some other stone on a flat-topped tree trunk, a dresser, bureau or coffee table. This action forms the altar itself where you will work with the tools of stone magic. Otherwise, any table will suffice.

Magical objects are often placed on the stone altar. These may be 'good luck charms' or power stones and metals, such as large quartz crystals, cross stones, staurolites, lodestones, fossils, lava and opals.

This area is the place to cleanse and purify stones, to attune with them and perform magic. Many of the spells mentioned in this book involve the use of candles as well as stones, and it is on the stone altar that these are placed and burned.

Incense, flowers and any other magical objects can be added to the stone altar as long as they are in tune with your magical need, or if you consider them to be 'power objects'—those things which increase or improve your ability to raise and send forth energy.

The stone altar is a place of magic.

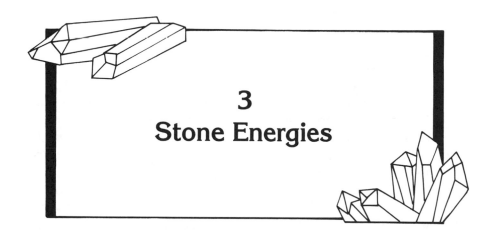

3
Stone Energies

A bewildering array of stones awaits our use in magic. They come in endless forms, crystalline shapes and colors. Their uses in magic are incredibly varied.

As I mentioned in Chapter One, stones are storehouses of energies. We utilize these energies in magic to bring about needed change.

There are two basic types of energy within stones. These two types contain all the various vibrations found in stones: those that attract love, repel negativity, and so on. These are the *projective* and the *receptive* energies.

They are manifestations of the purest forms of the universal energies that created everything. They have many symbols. In religion, they are known as God and Goddess. In astronomy, the Sun and the Moon. In humans, male and female.

Here are some more associations:

PROJECTIVE	RECEPTIVE
Electric	Magnetic
Hot	Cold
Day	Night
Physical	Spiritual
Bright	Dark

Projective	*Receptive*
Summer	Winter
Knife	Cup
Active	Inert

These powers are everywhere within the universe. They are present in our planet and ourselves. In magical thought they lie within our bodies. Symbolically speaking, this is why we can reproduce young of either sex and practice all forms of magic.

We contain both projective and receptive energies. These forces have nothing to do with our physical sex. Or rather, they shouldn't. But since we are trained from birth to stress that energy which conforms to our physical sex, imbalances are quite common. Boys are dressed in blue, taught to play baseball, wear pants and so on. Though this is changing today, it is still the norm.

One of the goals of the magician is to attain a perfect balance of these twin forces. When they become unbalanced, when one energy is more abundant or stressed, the magician follows suit.

An overabundance of projective energy makes the magician irritable, aggressive, angry and overly analytical. Healthwise this imbalance may lead to ulcers, headaches, high blood pressure and other maladies.

Too much receptive energy creates moodiness, lethargy, depression, disinterest and a shutting-out of the physical world. Other possible problems are nightmares, clinging love, lack of employment, depressed immuno-response and hypochondria.

When and if you notice an imbalance in your energy make-up, carry or wear stones of the opposite type to bring that force into play (see Part IV for a list of these stones).

That gets us back to the stones. The *projective stones* are those which are bright, outward, aggressive and electrical. They possess strong, forceful energies which deflect evil, overcome inertia and create movement.

Projective stones help destroy disease, strengthen the conscious mind, and imbue their wearer with courage and determination. They are used to promote physical energy, attract luck and bring success. In magic they might be used to add additional strength to rituals.

These rocks and minerals are used in two basic ways: to drive off unwanted, negative energies, or to put energies into an object or person. A woman wearing a carnelian for courage, for example, brings its energies into herself. The same woman wishing to deflect negativity from her body would empower the stone, through visualization, for this purpose. Thus, instead of sending energy into her, the stone sends it away from her. The secret, obviously, is in the visualization.

Projective stones contact the conscious mind. They are often heavy or dense, occasionally opaque, and are red, orange, yellow, gold or clear. They may also shine or gleam like the Sun. Examples of projective stones and minerals include ruby, diamond, lava, topaz, and rhodocrosite.

Projective stones are associated with the Sun, Mercury, Mars, Uranus and the elements of Fire and Air. (For more information on the elements see Part IV.) They are also related to the stars, since stars are simply distant suns.

Receptive stones are the natural complement of projective stones. They are soothing, calming, inward and magnetic, promoting meditation, spirituality, wisdom and mysticism. They create peace.

These stones promote communication between the conscious and subconscious minds, allowing psychic awareness to blossom. They radiate energies which attract love, money, healing and friendship. Receptive stones are often used for grounding purposes, to stabilize and reaffirm our Earth roots.

Like projective stones, the receptive ones are also used in two basic ways. Lapis lazuli can be used to draw love or, with different empowering, to absorb depression and thus create joy.

Receptive stones are found in a wide range of colors—green, blue, blue-green, purple, gray, silver, pink, black (the absence of color) and white (all colors combined). They may also be opalescent or translucent, and be naturally pierced with a hole.

Examples of receptive stones include moonstone, aquamarine, emerald, holey stones, rose quartz, pink tourmaline, kunzite, lapis lazuli and sugilite. They are linked with the Moon, Venus, Saturn, Neptune, Jupiter and the elements of Earth and Water.

Not all stones fit easily into one of these categories, but this is a good system to help us relate the stones to their basic powers. Some stones contain a mixture of these energies, like lapis lazuli. Others may have uses which belie this simple classification, so use your judgement in determining their basic powers. Remember, this is a system to be used for our benefit. It cannot be correct 100 percent of the time.

Just by looking at some unknown stone, by noticing its weight and color, you'll be able to know something about its magical properties even before trying to sense them.

The next time you see a stone—anywhere—try to determine whether it is receptive or projective. If this becomes an automatic process, you'll quickly learn the stones themselves and, in doing so, will discover stone magic becoming easier to practice.

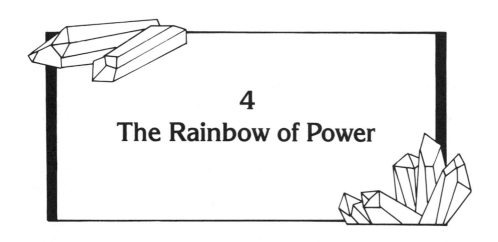

4
The Rainbow of Power

As I mentioned in the previous chapter, the colors of stones are a vital clue to unlocking their magical uses. Colors are energies with direct effects on our minds. As an example of this, many prisons now paint prisoner-holding areas a light pink hue. When aggressive criminals are placed in these rooms they become calm. Why? Pink is a soothing, loving color. The convicts, unless they're under the influence of mood-altering drugs, simply can't remain violent in such an environment.

Similarly, many hospitals are now painting surgery and recuperation rooms blue. This color has long been used in magic to promote healing, and now orthodox medicine is finally catching on.

The old magical systems are starting to be explained as we become more aware of the effects of color. If pink walls calm angry persons, why shouldn't stones of the same color be useful for attracting love?

Even on this superficial level, the colors that stones exhibit can have dramatic effects. When we use color as a key to other, less physical effects of stones, the realm of magic is truly entered.

The purpose of this section is to examine the basic colors of stones as well as their magical properties. Just as with Chapter Three, this information can act as a guide in discovering your own uses for stones as well as in understanding the information presented in Part II of this book.

This might be a good place to add some notes concerning magical healing. No one can heal another's body. Certainly there are techniques which facilitate this, but the healing must come from within. Most healers say that all they can do is speed up the process, perhaps by removing blockages in the energy flow through the sick person's body.

Stones have been used in healing magic for centuries, and some must have been effective. By presenting this traditional information in Part II of this book, I'm not telling you to grab a bloodstone when you cut your finger, or an emerald if you have eye troubles. I'm simply suggesting that such measures can be used *in conjunction with orthodox medical treatment.* So grab a bandage and antibacterial cream (or a plantain leaf) and dress the wound, *then* use a bloodstone to help speed your recovery.

Magic isn't a slap in the face of technology. It can and should be used with it whenever possible. Reading the 'healing' information in this book with this in mind should clear up any questions regarding this aspect of stone magic.

No doubt stones are powerful, but we must be knowledgeable about them, in harmony with them, and in touch with our own bodies for this magic to be effective.

Anyway, colors are powers. Colored stones are doubly powerful. Here are some of these energies.

Red

Red is the color of blood, of birth and death. In many cultures it has been 'sacred', or dedicated to the deities. Red stones are projective, active. They are related to the planet Mars and the element of Fire, both aggressive energies.

These are protective stones and work to strengthen the body and will power. Red stones are used to promote courage, to lend energy to the body, and to provide additional power to rituals by their presence on the altar.

In ancient times, red stones were worn as antidotes to poison, to keep one's thoughts 'pure', and, by drawing out the causes, to banish anger and all violent emotions. They were also used as a guard against fire and lightning.

In healing, red stones are intimately linked with blood. They are often worn to relieve anemia, to halt bleeding and to heal wounds.

They also seem to work on rashes and inflammation. Perhaps in association with its blood links, red stones were once carried to prevent miscarriage.

Red stones can be empowered and used to overcome sexual dysfunctions, usually by placing the stone near or on the genitals while visualizing.

Pink

Pink stones are receptive, packed with loving vibrations. They are calming, soothing, and are used to de-stress and relax the physical body as well as the mind.

Sometimes thought to be ruled by Venus (though green is a more Venusian color), pink stones are used to attract a love or to strengthen love already present. They may work to smooth over difficulties in long-standing relationships.

They can be worn to promote self-love. This isn't narcissism but a realization of your faults, acceptance and release of them, and then getting on with life. As I (and many others before me) have said, we cannot expect others to love us if we don't love ourselves. Pink stones are one energy we can utilize to achieve this.

Pink stones promote peace, happiness, joy and laughter. They stimulate the lighter emotions, help attract friends and encourage openness toward others.

They are ideal to utilize in group rituals.

Orange

Orange stones have some of the fire of red but are gentler in their effects. Projective, they have often been seen as symbols of the Sun. They are ideal for use in protective rituals and those designed to promote illumination.

These stones are related to personal power. Wearing one will enhance your ability to tap into and direct this energy during magical rites.

These are excellent stones to wear for those people with low self-esteem, for they expand your awareness of self-worth.

Orange stones are also thought to be luck-attracting, and as symbols of success, they are worn during spells to assure a positive outcome.

Yellow

Yellow stones and minerals are projective. Ruled by Mercury, they are used in rituals involving communication. If you're having trouble expressing yourself in an intelligible way, try wearing a yellow stone. Writers may receive help with their work by utilizing yellow stones, while public speakers wear them for eloquence.

Also ruled by the Sun, yellow stones are protective, while the element of Air, also a ruler, tells us that they can be used to strengthen the conscious mind. They are worn during magic to heighten visualization abilities.

Spells involving travel can be performed with yellow stones, perhaps by holding one in your projective hand and visualizing yourself traveling to your desired location.

Healthwise, yellow stones are used to promote digestion, to regulate the nervous system, and for skin problems.

These are stones of movement, of exchange, of energy and mental awareness.

Green

The color of nature, of fertility, of life, green has often been linked with red in religion and magic.

Stones of this hue are receptive. They are used in healing magic, perhaps by surrounding a green or blue candle with the gems, lighting the candle, and then visualizing the sick person as a vibrant, totally healed person.

They can also be carried or worn to guard the health. Specifically, green stones are thought to strengthen the eyes, control the kidneys, relieve stomach problems and prevent migraines.

Ruled by Venus, green stones are worn during gardening to promote luxuriant growth, or are placed in the earth for this purpose. If you have house plants, try putting a few empowered green stones in the earth. Due to such usage, they were also thought to increase fertility and therefore to promote conception.

Their associations with the element of Earth also lead to their use in spells involving money, riches, prosperity and luck.

They are grounding and balancing stones which can be worn to attune with the Earth.

Blue

Blue—the color of the ocean, of sleep, and of twilight. Ruled by the element of Water and the planet Neptune, these are receptive stones and promote peace. Holding a blue stone, or gazing at it by a soft light calms the emotions. If you have difficulty sleeping, try wearing blue stones to bed. This is also excellent for halting nightmares.

Blue stones are worn or used to promote healing, in general, and specifically to reduce fevers, remove ulcers and their causes, and for eliminating inflammations. They are sometimes held to reduce or remove pain from the body.

If you feel in need of a purification, wear blue stones, perhaps while bathing, to purify your inner being as well as your outer flesh. This is often done prior to magical ritual.

Purple

Stones which are purple or indigo-colored are receptive and spiritual. Ruled by Jupiter and Neptune, they have long been associated with mysticism and purification. These are excellent stones to wear for meditation, psychic work or during any ritual designed to contact the subconscious mind.

As with green and blue stones, purple is the color of healing and peace. These stones are worn to maintain health and are sometimes given to unruly children to promote obedience. Physically, purple stones are utilized to relieve complaints in the head such as headache, mental illness, concussion and hair problems. They relieve depression and produce restful sleep when worn at night.

Purple stones are associated with organized religion as well as the more spontaneous, Earth-oriented systems. They are worn to contact higher forces.

White

White stones are receptive and ruled by the Moon. As such they are intimately linked with sleep and psychism.

In the past, white stones, especially chalcedony, were worn to promote lactation by mothers having trouble feeding their babies. In contemporary America, these are considered to be lucky stones, often carried in the pocket or worn to promote good fortune.

Because the Moon glows at night, Her stones are used for protection after dark, often when walking alone in hazardous places. Sometimes white and red stones are carried or worn together for protection at all hours.

To be rid of a headache, carry a white stone in your pocket.

Some workers say that white stones, because they contain all colors, can be magically charged to act as substitutes for stones of any color. This is done through visualization.

Black

Black stones are receptive. They represent the Earth and stability and are ruled by Saturn, the planet of restriction. Black stones are symbolic of self-control, of resilience and quiet power.

They are sometimes viewed as protective, but black stones are more often used to 'earth' a person. If you're light-headed, dizzy, or so focused on the spiritual that your physical life suffers, wear black stones.

Mystically, black is the color of the outer spaces, of the absence of light. If you wish to perform a spell of magical invisibility, to ensure that your actions will not be noticed by others, use a black stone for this purpose. For example, make a small image of yourself out of black clay and adorn this with black stones. Place it in a black box or one made of mirrors, and then put the box in a dark place. This simply hides you from others if they represent a threat to your life.

Multicolored Stones

Stones which consist of various colors, such as bloodstone (green and red), tourmaline (many combinations) and the opal (all colors) are, obviously, more complex in their magical make-up than single-hued stones. For most of these, simply look at the colors individually and determine the stone's uses by combining the energies of each.

Opals are a special case, as are all stones which exhibit rainbows or a variety of colors. Check Part II of this book for specific information.

Other Colors

For those stones which contain flecks of metals, such as lapis lazuli (which contains iron pyrite), check Part III for information regarding the various metals within them.

Various shades or combinations of the basic colors listed above (such as lime green or turquoise) again require combining the information regarding each color.

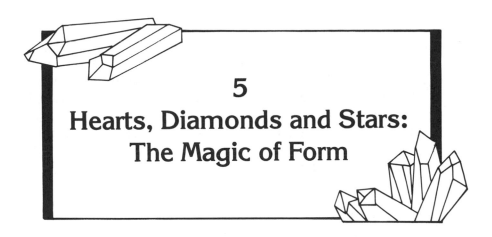

5
Hearts, Diamonds and Stars:
The Magic of Form

What special powers do gemstones such as the star ruby and star sapphire possess? Is a heart-shaped stone powerful in attracting love? What is the magical significance of round, square and triangular rocks?

Naturally created stones come in shapes from masses to hexagonal crystals. When they're exposed on the ground, wind and water action alters their appearance, often producing recognizable forms.

Or, when collected, they are broken up into smaller stones or extracted from the matrix in which they formed. Later, in the hands of a lapidary, they are tumbled and polished, cut and faceted; all of which obviously alter the stone's shape even further.

The forms of stones often reveal their magical powers to the knowledgeable observer. Those stones formed into familiar shapes by natural processes are thought to be more powerful than those artificially shaped. Such stones have deep magical significance.

This is shamanistic magic. In contemporary Peru shamans use such stones in their rituals. Various American Indian tribes prized animal-shaped stones for use in charms and rituals. However, the magic of stone forms is rarely considered today.

This chapter looks at some of the shapes in which gemstones are found, as well as those created by humans. It will also discuss those few stones which shimmer, gleam, and seem to have movement within them.

Since stones are found in many shapes, only the major ones will be examined here. If you find a peculiarly shaped stone, *let it speak to you*. What does it look like? What are your associations with that form? Sense its energies and work with it to discover its powers.

When working with naturally shaped stones, the type of stone isn't as important as its form, unless you decide it is.

In the shape lies the magic!

Round stones symbolize the receptive powers of the universe, of magnetism and the Mother Goddess. They are linked with the female reproductive system and indeed can be used to represent women in, for instance, healing rituals.

These stones are keys to spirituality, to unfolding psychic aware-ness. They are used in love spells and in all manner of 'attraction' rituals. An example: to attract money, place small pieces of olivine or jade in a square surrounding the round stone and visualize.

Spheres, now available in a wide range of stones, are often used in scrying sessions.

Long, thin stones are obvious phallic symbols, though this doesn't necessarily include quartz crystals or other crystalline stones. They are projective and represent electricity and the Great God of Pagan religions.

These are energy stones and can be carried or placed on the altar for this purpose. For protection hang one on the front door or place before a mirror.

Round and long stones can be used in conjunction for love spells by placing them beside or on top of each other on the altar while visualizing. Placing other love-attracting stones nearby, or surround-ing the two, furnishes additional power and symbolism to the ritual.

Stones that are *egg-shaped* are used to stimulate creativity and fresh ideas. They are also placed on the stone altar to bring 'fertility' to the ritual. In the past, small stones of this shape were carried by women to promote conception. Larger ones can be buried in the gar-den for fertile plants.

Square stones symbolize the Earth, prosperity and abundance, and so are used in spells of this type. They also promote stability and grounding. Use one of these to concentrate on one project at a time if you feel that your life is too scattered.

Heart-shaped stones are, of course, used magically to stimulate or draw love. They can be carried to bring love into your life or to magnify the love within, to allow yourself to receive and give love.

Triangular stones are protective and are worn or carried for this purpose. To guard your home, place a triangular stone in the window facing the nearest street.

Stones which are found in *L-shapes* are thought to bring good fortune, perhaps because this form suggests the conjunction of the spiritual with the physical. They can be carried as good luck pieces or placed on the altar.

Stones that resemble *parts of the body* are used in magic to heal or strengthen that particular part: kidney-shaped ones for the kidneys, and so on. These graphic stones, which are worn after the ritual, are focal points for visualization.

Pyramid-shaped stones, rare in nature but increasingly common among dealers, concentrate and release energies up through the tip toward the magical goal. Thus, if you need money, you might put a dollar bill beneath the pyramid and visualize money energy flowing from the bill up through the pyramid and out to bring you prosperity.

Diamond-shaped stones obviously recall that precious gem and so are used to attract riches.

These examples should be sufficient to allow you to explore the possible magical uses of the shaped stones you may find on beaches, river banks or in dry creek beds.

Holey stones, those with a naturally occurring hole, are so important in magic that they will be discussed in a separate section in Part II. Stones which naturally bear striking shapes such as staurolite and cross stone, will be found there also.

Other stones are prized not for their shapes, but for their shimmering or lustrous natures. Such stones as cat's eye, star ruby, star sapphire, moonstone, tiger's eye, sunstone and many others exhibit this phenomenon known as *chatoyancy*.

Numerous legends have formed around these stones. Some peoples believed that demons or spirits lived within them and caused the flashing effect.

Such stones have long been known to be protective, since they deflect negativity. They are worn as jewelry for personal protection. These "movement" stones are also beneficial for travel spells, or can be worn during journeys for their protective effects.

"Stars" appearing in sapphires and rubies are thought to increase the magical effectiveness of these stones.

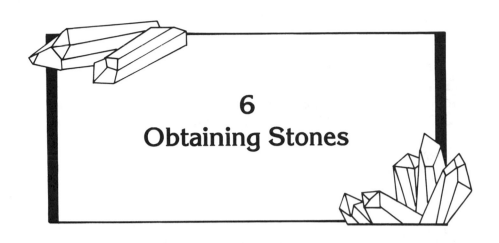

6
Obtaining Stones

Depending on your particular wants and needs, obtaining stones for magical purposes can be easy or difficult, inexpensive or costly.

You don't necessarily need gem quality stones for use in magic. Though a perfect emerald will have a strong magical effect, a lesser quality one (such as the emerald I bought at a rock show a few weeks ago for $4.50) will have the same effect, if slightly reduced in potency. So too will substitutions for such stones (see Part IV for a list of magical substitutions).

If you're serious about practicing stone magic, build up a stock of stones. You needn't obtain 100 different stones; ten or twelve will probably be adequate to begin with. Choose a selection that can be called upon for nearly any magical need. This is a representative selection:

Amethyst	Staurolite
Peridot	Amber
Lapis Lazuli	Quartz Crystal
Tiger's-eye	Rutilated Quartz
Garnet	Green, Pink, Blue and
Carnelian	Black Tourmaline

Your own needs and areas of interest will affect your choice, of course. Read Part II of this book and compose a personal list. Alter this as you discover new stones or come upon unexpected situations where you need them.

How do you get the stones themselves? There are three basic methods: buying, bartering, and collecting. While most stones are bought and paid for today (just as in the past), it's cheaper and more fun to barter for stones. Collecting them fresh from the Earth is better still.

BUYING STONES

The range of stones available today is staggering. They come from all over the world, often traveling tens of thousands of miles, and pass through many hands before ending up at the counter where you pay for them. They may cost pennies each for common or lesser-quality specimens. Other stones will fetch hundreds or thousands of dollars per gram or carat.

Most large cities have rock shops, and small towns in mineral-rich areas have them as well. Though the proprietors will seldom have much firsthand knowledge of magic, these are still great places to "hang out," buy stones, and learn about their non-occult properties. Their prices will often be excellent but shop around for the best values. Once you've made contact with the owners of rock shops, you'll learn when new stones are expected in the store and may have first pick of them.

Metaphysical, New Age or occult supply stores usually carry a variety of stones. These stores are found in increasing numbers across the country. Virtually every one sells quartz crystals, the "new" stone for the New Age.

Check the phone book for local suppliers of rocks and gemstones.

Natural history museums sell stones in their gift shops, usually at good prices. County fairs with exhibits by local gem or rock clubs will often have sale areas as well.

Mail-order sources are also available for stones; I've listed these in the Appendix of this book.

And finally, local or regional gem shows offer an overwhelming array of specimens for your perusal.

Gem or rock shows are an established part of the trade. These are "rituals" that attract thousands of collectors and hundreds of merchants. The show itself—often housed in a convention center—consists of endless rows of booths, each occupied by a dealer. Hundreds of thousands of gemstones and minerals shine in the light.

You'll find your best buys at rock shows. Many of the dealers who travel around the country from show to show are well aware of the local merchants, and so the prices are competitive. To ensure that you don't overpay for a stone, check several dealers before making your purchase.

When I began practicing magic in 1971, much was made of an "old" magical edict. It states: don't barter or haggle over objects obtained for magic. This was interpreted to include looking for the best possible price. In the past few years, this seems to have been forgotten and is rarely mentioned in conversations or books. Though I once followed this "rule," I always felt—as others did—that it was formulated or popularized by merchants eager to get the highest prices for their wares.

So much for the haggling rule! It is no longer current. Money is energy in a physical form. Though I don't perform magic for pay, I don't see anything wrong with using money intelligently when purchasing magical objects, including stones.

Back to the shows. Stones virtually unobtainable in local shops are often uncovered at rock shows. Ask the merchants for the unusual stone and you just might find it. At a recent show in San Diego, I looked in vain for sunstone and staurolite. Just inquiring about them at two different stalls produced fine examples which I quickly bought.

Rock shows are produced all over the country. For news of upcoming events, check the listings in the current *Lapidary Journal* (see Appendix: Stone Sources) or your local newspaper. Ask at rock shops too; the owners are often aware of shows that occur in nearby areas.

BARTERING FOR STONES

Don't have much money, but an excess of one type of stone? Why not try bartering? Exchanging one object of value for another object of similar value is an ancient practice, far older than the use of money.

In earlier times magicians and Witches weren't paid for healings, purifications, other magical rituals or psychic work. They were given food, shelter, or other necessities in exchange for the energy expended. This system is still in use in primitive lands and also in industrialized countries.

If you have friends who are interested in expanding the range of their stone collections, especially ones involved in magic, get your stones together and see what comes up.

Bartering is a particularly satisfying form of exchange. It increases your range of stones and that of your friends. No money is exchanged, thus lessening the immediate economic impact of broadening the type of stones you can use in magic. It is quite common among collectors who go out and dig their own, which leads us to the third method of obtaining stones.

COLLECTING STONES

What an adventure it is to collect stones and minerals. Brushing away dirt and seeing a brilliant flash of color is an exhilarating, magical experience. Buying stones is certainly exciting but finding your own is more satisfying.

Throughout the world there are rich collecting areas for various gemstones and minerals. Living in San Diego, I'm fortunate to have nearby areas offering tourmaline, kunzite, garnet, lepidolite, mica, beryl, quartz crystal, agate and calcite among many other stones and minerals. Good collection sites can be found virtually everywhere on the globe.

As magicians working with the natural forces of the universe, and respecting the Earth as a manifestation of these forces, it is only right to approach a collecting trip with reverence. Rituals and offerings made before setting out are often thought of as mandatory by magical practitioners.

Besides the sheer fun of it, and the awe of discovering stones never before seen by human eyes, there are other reasons for gathering your own stones.

Much bad feeling currently surrounds the strip mining of quartz crystals in Arkansas. Strip mining is the least expensive and most Earth-damaging way to gather the crystals. Around the world, poor laborers work from dawn to dusk extracting valuable gemstones for unscrupulous mine owners, who pay them pennies for collecting stones that may fetch thousands of dollars. Stone prices are often fixed and kept at artificially high rates, thereby denying many of us the simple pleasure of owning them as well as access to their powers.

Due to such situations as these, some magicians are questioning the value of some of the stones found on the market. Are the powers inside a quartz crystal that's been ripped out of the ground negative? Is an emerald collected by a sweating, undernourished Columbian worker magically tainted?

Some workers say yes and recommend such stones be specially prepared and purified before use in magic and ritual. Since gemstones can be 'programmed' much like computers, any ill feeling or misuse involved in their collection can be imprinted on them and affect their final owner.

To be free of doubts about the origin, authenticity and the method of collection of the stones, try gathering your own. This is a simple process. Check local bookstores (especially those in museums), libraries or rock shops for guides on nearby collecting areas. Many working mines have special days set aside for collectors to do their own mining or, more often, dig through the *tailings*—the remains of the miner's work, which are often rich in gemstones. A small fee is usually required for liability insurance.

There are also many collecting areas on state or federal land that are open for use by rockhounds. Those on national parks are, of course, taboo, while sites lying on private property require advance permission from the owner.

Plan your trip so as to be prepared for all conditions—rain (wet gear), blinding sun (sunblock, sunglasses and a wide-brimmed hat) and snake bite (first-aid kit). Also bring food and water and anything else you can think of. Bring along a friend too. If you're going into isolated areas, tell friends where you're headed and when you plan to be back.

Simple tools—a trowel, pickax, small shovel, screens for sifting through dirt, small bags, bottles or vials to contain your specimens, perhaps a brush and a knife—are all you'll need, along with a larger bag or a backpack to carry everything. Caves and mines require hard hats, rope, high-intensity flashlights and protective clothing.

Once you're prepared for your collecting trip, perform some sort of ritual to the Earth. This needn't be anything more than an attunement, an offering, and an advance thanks. Since there are endless varieties of such pre-collection rituals, here are two examples.

The first is performed prior to leaving on your trip.

Stand before your stone altar. In your right hand hold a specimen (if you have one) of the type of stone you'll be searching for. Attune with it and, through it, with the Earth. Visualize huge caverns filled with glistening crystals. Feel the stones vibrating within the earth, emitting or absorbing energies.

Visualize yourself finding the stones. In any words or symbols thank the Earth for its sacrifice. While doing this, carry the stone outside and bury it in the earth, anywhere.

It is done.

The next example can be performed upon arrival at the site or outside before traveling to the area.

Select some precious object—a polished gemstone, a small silver coin, a few drops of a costly oil, some wine or honey. Go out of doors to a place wild and lone or to the actual collecting site.

Sit on the Earth and place your hands on it on either side of your thighs. Straighten your spine until you are upright and yet comfortable.

Feel the Earth vibrating beneath you. Call to it, ask it for its permission to gather stones. Visualize yourself lovingly gathering the stones. See yourself using them in positive, life-affirming magic.

Then bury your offering in the soil and, with a reverent attitude, begin your journey or collection.

How effective are such rituals?

One friend said that whenever he performed such a rite before collecting he had good results, but when he omitted it, the reverse occurred. Such rituals certainly aren't *necessary*. Those rockhounds uninvolved in magic would never think to do such things and yet make fabulous finds.

For those of us working in magic, however, they are a prerequisite. We are not here to 'dominate and subdue the Earth'. We work in harmony with it, especially when garnering some of its treasures.

So perform your ritual and collect your own magical stones. And happy digging!

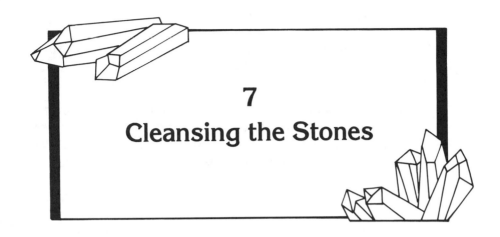

7
Cleansing the Stones

As I mentioned in Chapter Six, stones are subject to a wide range of energies before they arrive in your home. Prior to using them in magic, many practitioners perform a cleansing or purification on the stones.

This is a simple process which removes any past influences from the stone, readying it for our uses. It is advisable to do this for each stone. The only exceptions are those which you yourself have collected unless you found them near a military institution, a highway or polluted ground.

There are a number of methods of stone purification. The simplest is to place the stones in full sunlight for a day, three days, or even a week. The Sun's rays do the work here, burning away the unnecessary energies.

Place the stones in direct sunlight. An inside window ledge isn't as good as an outdoor location because window glass blocks some of the Sun's rays. Remove the stones each day at dusk.

Some stones will be 'clear' after a day's soaking up the rays. Others will need longer periods of time. Check the stones daily and sense the energies within them by placing them in your receptive hand. If the vibrations are regular, healthy, the cleansing has been successful.

A second method is somewhat more difficult. In this case, running water is the tool. Place the stones in moving water and leave them there for a day or two.

If you happen to have a river or stream running near your property, this is ideal. Place the stones in a net bag or devise some other method to ensure that they don't wash away in the water. Leave them overnight in the water, which gently washes away the impurities.

The third main technique is governed by the powers of the Earth. Bury the stone in the ground for a week or so, then check to see if it has been purified. If it has, wash or wipe it off and your magic can begin.

These are all natural purifications, performed with the energies of the elements. If you can't do them, however, there is another method, a ritual of purification, which can be performed in your own home. Perform this rite on your altar, if you have one, or on any table. It is best done at sunrise or during the day.

Fill a basin with pure water and place this to the West on the table or altar.

Next, light a red candle and set this to the South. Light some incense and place this to the East.

Finally, place a dish or flowerpot filled with freshly dug earth to the North on the altar. In between all these objects set the stone to be purified.

When all is readied, still your mind and pick up the stone in your projective hand. Turn your attention toward the bowl of earth. Place the stone on it and cover with fresh earth. Say something to the effect of:

I purify you with Earth!

Leave the stone there for a few minutes, all the while visualizing the earth absorbing the stone's impurities.

Then remove it, dust it clean, and hold it in the incense smoke. Pass it nine times through the smoke, from the right to the left, saying words like these:

I purify you with Air!

See the smoke wafting away the disturbing energies.

Next, quickly pass the stone through the candle's flame several times, saying:

I purify you with Fire!

The fire burns away all negativity.

Now place the stone in the water and say this or your own words:

I purify you with Water!

Visualize the water washing it clean.

Leave the stone in the water for a time, then dry it with a clean cloth and hold it in your receptive hand.

Is the stone 'clean'? If not, repeat this simple ritual as many times as necessary, until you are sure it has done its work.

Afterward, store the stone in a special place. It is ready for use in magic.

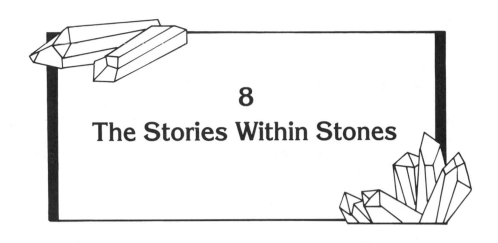

8
The Stories Within Stones

It's best to get to know stones before using them in magic. Becoming familiar with them allows you to work with their powers. After attuning with, say, an amethyst, you'll develop a 'magical knowledge' concerning that stone. This is a true tool and is one of the three necessities of magic. (See Chapter Two.)

Meditate on ten or so stones to begin with, and add more later as they come into your life, as sugilite recently entered mine. When a situation requiring a magical rite occurs, you'll know the stone to use.

Work with the stones individually. If you study citrine, say, in the morning and switch to aventurine in the afternoon, your associations with these stones won't be as clear as if you'd split your session over two days, allowing for more in-depth study of each.

Try to repeat sessions on each stone at least two or three times in the same day, for full immersion. If nothing else, after your main attunement, simply look at the stone a few times throughout the day, or hold it for a moment.

To 'hear' the stories within stones, you might try a method like the following. It is designed, in the best shamanistic sense, to allow the stone to teach you. The universe is constantly speaking to us, to all of us. Remember to listen!

Cleanse the stone if necessary (see Chapter Seven). Then set aside a time, say a half-hour to an hour, depending on your desire to work with stones.

Find a quiet spot. It may be in your garden, the living room when the rest of the household is asleep, or a quiet valley in a nearby forest. Even a city park or a rooftop will do. Ideally, any outdoor location is preferable to in-home working but, again, do what you can.

This is a two-section stone exercise. The first one utilizes the psychic, subconscious, deep conscious mind. At least a part of this has lately been dubbed the "right brain." The second utilizes the intellectual, conscious, societally controlled mind, now known by some as the "left brain."

Settle down comfortably before the stone on the ground, floor, or in a chair at a table. The stone should be within arm's reach. Close your eyes and listen to your own mantra, your breath. Still your conscious mind. Breathe deeply, rhythmically.

With your eyes still closed, hold out your receptive hand (the left hand for righties, the right for left-handers). Keeping it a few inches from the floor, move it back and forth gently. Pinpoint your concentration or your awareness on the palm of this hand. You are searching for the stone. Don't *try* to feel the stone's energies; *simply allow yourself to do so.*

Say I was doing this with a small quartz crystal. As my hand passes over it, I might feel a strong emanation rising from the stone, perhaps manifesting as a warm, throbbing spot on my palm.

When I move my hand away from the crystal, the feeling stops. Passing over it once again, the energy stream moves through my palm. This may seem strange or supernatural, but it's a perfectly natural use of our senses, and it is vital in magic.

When you have located the stone, pick it up, again using your senses to determine the exact location of the stone. Your fingers should close around it perfectly. If not, work on it again.

Your eyes are still shut. You are utilizing the psychic mind. Hold the stone in your receptive hand for a while. The energies will be easier to detect now that you are closer to their source. How do they feel?

Do they affect your mood? Are you happier? Calmer? Energized? Aroused?

With your eyes still closed, move the stone slowly up and down a few inches from your body from your belly to the top of your head. Do you feel anything different?

Do you feel the energy of the stone within you, almost like a warm ray of sunshine? Or a cool ray of moonlight?

Next, transfer the stone to your projective hand. Feel the stone. Is it smooth, glossy, rough, or striated (rippled or grooved)? Does it crumble? Is it cold to the touch? Warm?

Once you've surveyed it with your fingers, sense the stone's weight. Is it light? Heavy?

Remember all this—all impressions, sensations, and emotional effects, if any.

Open your eyes and look at the stone. With all the information you've just received in mind, study it with your eyes. You've certainly looked at the stone before, but never with all these sensations.

Gaze at it for a while, perhaps, simply seeing it—for the first time. See it with a shaman's eyes. Penetrate it with your vision, analyze it, flex your conscious mind.

What shape is it? If it hasn't been worked by a lapidary, is it a smooth, natural crystal, a rough chunk of mineral or a water-buffed stone? If it is crystalline, how many sides does it contain? Are they regular or unevenly shaped? Smooth or deeply grooved?

Now focus on the stone's color, letting it fill your consciousness. Is the shade intense or pale? Bright or dark? Pleasing or discomforting? Does it affect your mood? What are your associations, magical or otherwise, with the color?

Is the stone solidly opaque, translucent, or transparent?

Let the stone answer these questions. Study the stone as a doctor would a patient. The stone has been speaking to you, revealing its magical nature and uses.

When you feel your concentration wavering, or when you are simply bored (a good sign that the 'conversation' is over), and especially if you're interrupted, hold the stone with both hands, move it up to the sky, move it down to the ground, and then press it against your belly. This is a simple ritual defining the end of the session, utilizing a symbolic presentation of the stone to all the energies above and below.

Now look up magical information relating to the stone in this or other books. See if it agrees with what you've discovered.

If you're the type that likes to record things, write a summary of the session. Note the stone, its energies, your feelings.

If you wish, carry or wear the stone for a few hours during the day or night after your attunement. Sense any changes within yourself while wearing the stone.

Otherwise, put the stone in a safe place, perhaps on your altar or, if you have one, in your power bag. (See the Glossary for any unfamiliar terms used in this book.)

Your stone meditation is finished.

Again, do this as many times a day as you feel necessary. It might take only one session for you to process all this information, but it may take several. You might try doing the 'conscious' half of this exercise during the day and the 'subconscious' half at night. *Sunset* or *sunrise* are ideal times to perform this, for they symbolize the shift from the psychic mind (night) to the analytical mind (day).

If you have friends who use stones in magic, ask them about their impressions of the stones. Share information, if you wish, for no one has a monopoly on such matters. Remember that others' impressions may be far different from yours.

Sure, this may seem complicated. After all, won't the stone do its magical work without such a ritual? Perhaps it would. Certainly it does, sometimes. But in stone magic, the powers we sense in the raw materials are only part of the energies we use. Stones are often used as focal points for *personal power*, which we rouse within our bodies.

Through ritual we release this personal power into the stones, which act like lenses that focus and concentrate the energy while adding their own to the 'transmission'. The energy is then sent out toward the magical goal.

Our intimate knowledge of stones, of their form, color, and powers, gives us a firmer connection with them, allowing a surer, stronger projection of energy into them. Perhaps stone magic will work without the magician's familiarity with the tools. But just as practice and desire can turn a whittler into an accomplished wood-carver, so too can sessions such as these determine the effectiveness of the practitioner's magic. To skip them is to miss half the magic.

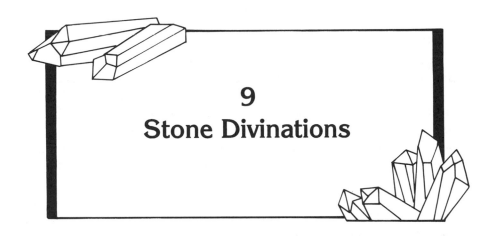

9
Stone Divinations

Divination is a magical process which utilizes various tools to provide glimpses of the future. The use of tarot cards is a form of divination, as is watching clouds pass overhead or gazing at the patterns caused by tea leaves in a cup.

For those of us who are unable to be consciously psychic when the need arises, divination is the next best thing. While performing this magic, we focus our conscious mind on the symbols presented to us and allow them to contact our psychic mind. The symbols—coins, rune stones, raindrops on a window—are simply keys which enable us to unlock our psychic awareness.

There are thousands of forms of divination. It has been practiced in all cultures throughout history. Sometimes these rites were performed by the individual, sometimes by priestesses, priests or shamans. The quest for knowledge of possible future events is still alive today.

I said "possible future events" above because nothing is carved in stone. The future isn't mapped out in advance; our lives aren't unfolding according to some divine plan. We are creating our futures every second of every day. Our lives are the results of our decisions.

Just as we determine our futures, other persons can influence our lives as well if we allow them to. Universal forces ebb and flow, adding their energy to the shape of tomorrow. The factors that are at work here are incomprehensible.

Fortunately, we needn't understand these processes to gain a glimpse of the future. All we need do is choose our tools and use them ritually to contact the psychic awareness that exists within us all.

Stone divination is an excellent form of this ancient art. When you need guidance regarding an important decision, look to stones for help. If fear grips you when you think about an upcoming event, look to stones. If you're unsure whether the magical rite you're about to perform is designed for your goal, use a stone divination to bring all sharply into focus.

This can easily become a crutch. The man or woman who won't leave the house without consulting a psychic is a cliché, but it is too often true. Divination isn't divine guidance or a necessity for daily living; it is a tool which we pick up and use when needed, then set down. Divination can help us make decisions, warn us of possible dangers or ill-health, and provide another perspective on a problem.

It may be exciting to perform a divination, but it should never be done "just for fun" or out of boredom. Like magic, divination is used when it is necessary.

Most divinatory systems contain some sort of element of 'chance'. This determines which tools—in this case, stones—will be available to help us unlock the secrets of tomorrow. Pulling a stone at random from a bag, shuffling tarot cards, or tossing I Ching stalks or coins brings chance into the divination. In a sense we allow the universe (nature, Deity) to determine which stone or card is best suited to help us in our quest.

Other forms of divination rely on more direct communication with the subconscious mind. The pendulum, for example, is a tool which is set in motion by miniscule movements of the arm and hand that hold it. These movements are caused by the psychic mind and are interpreted to gain an answer.

Some types of divination utilize both of these systems.

If you're consciously psychic at will, you won't need divination. If not, you may want to begin working with one of the systems outlined in this chapter. In doing so, remember these things:

It may take a few sessions for you to properly work the divination, to approach it with the correct frame of mind, and to use the symbols presented to you to unfold your psychic awareness.

The future isn't predetermined. If you see something that bothers you, change it through magic! If an unreasonably rosy picture is presented to you, you might question yourself: Am I reading my desires into this? Am I properly utilizing the system? Is this system appropriate for me? (In other words, does it speak to my psychic mind?)

Divination is performed out of necessity. If an honest conversation, a few phone calls or letters, or a few moments of concentration will successfully clear up your questions, try these things first. If not, work with your stones.

STONE SCRYING

Scrying—gazing into or contemplating a shining, luminous or reflective surface.

Stone scrying is probably the best-known form of divination. Reflective, highly polished stones have been used for millennia in developing psychic awareness.

Most people have heard of the ubiquitous 'crystal ball'. This magical tool is simply a sphere of quartz crystal. Large, clear quartz spheres can cost $1,000 to $10,000; but smaller ones an inch or less in size are available for about $20.00 The six-inch variety seen in cheap movies are made of glass or plastic. The six-inch quartz spheres are rare and costly but, fortunately, aren't necessary.

Quartz isn't the only stone chosen for scrying. A multitude of other stones are also used for forms of scrying. Flat, square pieces of obsidian were favored in ancient Mexico and beryl spheres or eggs were the stones of choice during the Renaissance, but the crystal sphere captured the popular imagination long ago.

This is a guide for those interested in scrying with quartz crystal spheres. Remember, this is a *guide* only. As with everything in magic, do what your intuition tells you to do.

After obtaining your sphere, wash it in water. Dry and wrap in *black, yellow* or *white* cloth.

Traditionally, spheres used for scrying are never exposed to sunlight, as this is thought to hinder its ability to contact the psychic mind. Perhaps it would if you believed it would.

However, moonlight is used to purify crystal spheres. The Full Moon is an ideal time to cleanse and 'charge' a crystal with your magical intent—in this case, successful scrying. Take the wrapped sphere out into the moonlight. Unwrap it, and, with both hands, hold it up to the Moon.

Feel its cool light raining down on you. See it (through visualization) flooding the crystal, attuning it with your energy. Then visualize yourself successfully scrying with the sphere.

After a few moments wrap the sphere again. It is done.

As for the scrying itself, here are a few pointers:

It is best done at night. Symbolism is certainly at work here: night rules the psychic mind. Also, there's probably less chance of interruption.

Find a quiet spot. Sit comfortably. Place the crystal on a stand on a table or hold it in your hands.

Candlelight can be conducive to scrying. Though some say that reflections of the flames in the crystal are disturbing, for others this is exactly what helps them achieve the proper state.

Experiment to see what works best for you. You might place white or yellow candles behind your back at first, then move them to either side of you, and finally ring the crystal itself with the candles.

Once you, the crystal and the candles are all situated, relax. Breathe deeply for a few moments with your eyes closed. Forget the worries of the day, the stresses, the problems. Relax your body; relax your mind.

Then open your eyes and hold the crystal in your hands until it is warm. Some magicians say that stones won't work in magic unless this is done. As your hands warm the stone, your body is releasing personal power into the stone. Visualize your area of inquiry during this process.

Now replace the stone on the stand or continue holding it, whichever you feel comfortable with.

Continue to relax; gaze into the crystal. Don't stare unblinkingly into its depths, simply gaze. Blink your eyes if you wish. You must be calm and relaxed during scrying.

The crystal is a symbol of psychism, of Water (the psychic element), of your need to divine the future. Hold these things in mind as you gaze into the sphere.

If the operation is successful, you will contact your psychic mind and communication between it and your conscious awareness will take place.

Will you see pictures? Probably not—the crystal isn't a movie screen. You may see wisps of smoke swirling within the sphere—this is common. But few see images within it.

No. If anywhere, you'll see them in your mind. Images seen during scrying are often symbolic; they aren't psychic news footage of future events. Interpret the symbolism as best you can.

If you see no pictures, unbidden thoughts may come into your mind instead. Words, phrases or complete sentences may 'pop up' out of your psychic mind.

Whatever you see or think—either images within the sphere or in your mind, or words or phrases—try to relate them to your question or your area of inquiry.

Words are simple enough. Think about them. Do they mean anything to you? Are they ambiguous or direct?

Symbols are more difficult. For example, if you were asking if it would be a positive action to move to a new home, and you saw images of bats flying above slithering snakes, then interpret these symbols.

To some, snakes are related to wisdom and bats to luck. For such a person, the move would seem to be favorable. However, if you fear snakes and find bats disgusting, your symbols are suggesting the opposite.

See how it works? Symbols are the language of the subconscious mind, and, while we may all speak the same language, we use different dialects. Thus, the psychic mind uses a personal language which may mean nothing to others.

If you can't find or afford a crystal sphere, or don't wish to use one, there are several other methods of stone scrying. Any naturally reflective stone, most crystals, and those which seem to possess inner movement can be used as 'mirrors of the psychic mind'. These last stones include cat's-eye, moonstone, sunstone, tiger's-eye, star ruby, opal and many others.

Take the stone out into sunlight or moonlight, or hold it near a candle. Still your conscious mind. Move the stone slowly in your hands while visualizing your area of inquiry.

Do this for several minutes. Don't *will* anything to happen; simply wait until the strange movements in the stone and the hypnotic movements of your hands break your conscious mind's hold on psychic input.

Again, interpret any symbols you may see.

FIFTY-STONE DIVINATION

This is an entirely different form of stone divination. Though I'd love to have fifty emeralds to use for this ritual, the type of stone used isn't important. If financially practical, select psychism-inducing stones such as amethyst, aquamarine, citrine, quartz crystal, moonstone, in any combination. Or use whatever you have. Since the universe (chance, Goddess, Being, or God) provides the answer to your inquiry, there are no symbols to interpret.

Yes, this divination is limited and shouldn't necessarily be taken seriously, but it just may provide the answers you need.

Fill a bag or box with fifty stones of approximately the same size. Think of your question and reach into the bag and grab a handful of stones.

Place these on a flat surface before you and count the number of stones you have randomly chosen.

Odd numbers indicate favorable conditions, a positive answer, success. Even numbers presage the reverse.

RAINBOW STONE DIVINATION

This divination uses the colors of stones to provide clues regarding the future. You'll need seven stones, one of each color, all approximately the same size and shape. Place these in a soft cloth bag, and, when you need guidance, select a stone at random from the bag. It may answer your questions. If not, take another stone and 'read' or interpret them together.

Here's a list of recommended stones, along with their suggested divinatory meanings. But remember: these are generally accepted associations with the colors. If they don't speak to you, find your own or correct my list.

RED: ruby, red jasper, red agate, rhodonite, red tourmaline, garnet. Symbolizes anger or other destructive emotions, birth, change, sex, passion, endings, energy, confrontations.

PINK: pink tourmaline, rose quartz, pink calcite, rhodocrosite, kunzite. Symbolizes love, friendship, peace, joy, relationships, family, interchange.

ORANGE: carnelian, amber, citrine, tiger's-eye. Symbolizes illumination, personal power, energy, growth.

YELLOW: yellow tourmaline, topaz, yellow fluorite. Symbolizes protection, communication, travel, movement, exchange.

GREEN: jade, peridot, olivine, aventurine, emerald, green tourmaline.

Symbolizes growth, money, grounding, health, fertility, business, transactions.

BLUE: celestite, aquamarine, sodalite, blue quartz, blue tourmaline, turquoise, sapphire. Symbolizes peace, sleep, healing, purification, emotions, subconscious.

PURPLE: sugilite, lepidolite, amethyst. Symbolizes spirituality, evolution, mysticism, expansion, reincarnation.

How do you interpret these stones? I'll give an example.

Say I'm wondering what's causing me to be so depressed lately. I've been down for weeks and can't figure out why.

So I still my mind, and then get my bag of stones and reach inside.

I pull out a green stone. The first thing that flashes into my mind is money. Wanting more input, I pull out a red stone. 'Energy' passes through my mind as I look at it. Money and energy. But I asked about depression.

Could I have been depressed all this time because I wasn't making enough money? No, not that. Could it be that I haven't been putting enough energy (work) into making the money I earn? That could be. I analyze it, and it seems right.

I've found a possible reason for my depression. Now what do I do?

Use magic to change my condition. Transform a negative into a positive. Working more will help, but using magic will help even more. I might wish to carry or wear the green and red stones to push me further toward what I should be doing.

See?

It isn't always this simple, but try it out. Work with this or any system to receive its greatest gifts.

10
A Stone Tarot

The tarot—a mystic book, a tool of divination, a pack of cards. The tarot is perhaps more popular today than it has ever been, and new decks seem to be released every week. Collecting them makes a fine, if expensive, hobby.

Chapter Nine outlined some forms of divination utilizing stones. This chapter describes a more complex form—a veritable 'stone tarot'.

This is like the more familiar form except that, rather than using symbol-packed cards to point to future trends, the stones themselves contain this symbolism. Thus, instead of interpreting the situation by studying the symbolism of the cards, the reader studies the stones, recalling their symbolism.

In general, this type of stone tarot relates to the major arcana of the most popular decks, such as the Rider-Waite. I have tried to eliminate most of the Christian influences on this deck, using earlier associations and names for the "cards."

In particular, this system is symbolically associated with Wicca. The third tarot trump, known elsewhere as the Empress, is here termed the Goddess. An olivine, peridot, turquoise or one of their magical substitutions is used for this trump. The Goddess represents the moist, female, nurturing, creative aspect of the universal force— the receptive energies. The Goddess is one-half of the deity orientation of Wicca, the other being the God, here represented by a ruby and related to the Emperor card of the Rider-Waite deck.

This stone tarot consists of twenty-two stones. It's best to obtain stones that are the same approximate size, though you don't have to mortgage the house to buy a huge emerald to match your quarter-sized rose quartz. Polished and tumbled stones are best for this use, but crystals can be used as well.

If you don't agree with some of my associations between the stones and the cards, fine. Make your own system.

Obtain all twenty-two stones (you cannot work this magical tool without the full number) and cleanse each. If any are unfamiliar to you, work with them as outlined in Chapter Seven until you know their symbolism and magical uses.

Once you've done this, read over the divinatory information contained in this chapter for each stone. Attune with one stone at a time, relating the information to the stone itself. It's best not to begin working this tarot until after you know each stone. Sure, you can look up the meanings I've included in this chapter, but such forms of divination are second best. Relying on the written word during a reading is limiting. When you glance down at the stones, the overall picture they're presenting should 'flash' in your mind.

As you see each stone, recall its divinatory meaning. Look at its proximity to other stones, its relative position. It is this information which unlocks your psychic awareness, allowing you to find an answer, clear up a situation, or determine possible future events.

When not in use, keep the stones in a *yellow* cloth bag or some other suitable container. Expose them periodically to moonlight.

Wearing psychic-influencing stones such as lapis lazuli, moonstone, azurite or others may help you tap into your psychic awareness. If you wish, burn yellow candles and sandalwood incense while casting the stones. Anoint yourself with a similar oil, such as tuberose, nutmeg, lemon grass or sandalwood.

Eventually, the way of the stones and their messages will come easily, and you'll be able to perform a stone tarot reading with little difficulty. It can work!

For quick reference, here's a list of the major arcana and their associated stones. Remember, I've changed the names of some of these trumps, but their basic meanings are similar to the standard ones. I've included the more usual names in parentheses.

0. **THE FOOL** . . . . *AGATE*

1. **THE SHAMAN (MAGICIAN)** . . . . *QUARTZ CRYSTAL*

2. **THE HIGH PRIESTESS** . . . . *EMERALD, PEARL*

3. **THE GODDESS (EMPRESS)** . . . . *PERIDOT, OLIVINE,*
   TURQUOISE

4. **THE GOD (EMPEROR)** . . . . *RUBY*

5. **THE CHIEF (HIEROPHANT)** . . . . *TOPAZ*

6. **THE LOVERS** . . . . *ROSE QUARTZ*

7. **THE ELEMENTS (CHARIOT)** . . . . *STAUROLITE,*
   CROSS STONE, ANY
   TWINNED CRYSTALS

8. **STRENGTH** . . . . *DIAMOND,*
   HERKIMER
   DIAMOND, GARNET

9. **THE WISE ELDER (HERMIT)** . . . . *SAPPHIRE, BLUE*
   TOURMALINE

10. **THE SPIRAL (WHEEL OF FORTUNE)** *SARDONYX,*
    BLACK OPAL

11. **JUSTICE** . . . . *CARNELIAN*

12. **INITIATION (HANGED MAN)** . . . . *BERYL,*
    AQUAMARINE

13. **CHANGE (DEATH)** . . . . *AMBER*

14. **TEMPERANCE** . . . . *AMETHYST*

15. **FOLLY (DEVIL)** . . . . *BLACK DIAMOND,*
    BLACK
    TOURMALINE,
    ANY SQUARE
    BLACK STONE

16. **FORCE (THE TOWER)** . . . . *LODESTONE, LAVA*

17. **THE STAR** . . . . *METEORITE, ANY*
    STAR STONE

18. **THE MOON** . . . . *MOONSTONE,*
    CHALCEDONY

19. **THE SUN** . . . . *TIGER'S-EYE,*
    SUNSTONE

20. **REBIRTH (JUDGEMENT)** . . . . *FOSSIL*

21. **THE UNIVERSE** . . . . *OPAL, KUNZITE*

I have listed one or two recommended stones above. For those stones you cannot obtain, any of their magical substitutes can be used, provided that they aren't used to represent any other card. For example, though the peridot is a substitute for the emerald, you wouldn't want to use it for the High Priestess if you've already allocated it to the Goddess.

SYMBOLISM AND DIVINATORY MEANINGS OF STONE TAROT

0. THE FOOL - AGATE. Scattered energies, extravagance, waste, "head in the clouds," imbalance, pride, ego, hubris, vanity.

1. THE SHAMAN - QUARTZ CRYSTAL. Magical attainment, control, power, balance, center, unification of spiritual and physical, self-knowledge, depth, confidence.

2. THE HIGH PRIESTESS - EMERALD, PEARL. Spirituality, secrets, power, Earth religion, the unknown, female mysteries.

3. THE GODDESS - PERIDOT, OLIVINE, TURQUOISE. Receptive energy, women, cycles, fertility, creativity, abundance, growth, love, female sexuality, money, mother.

4. THE GOD - RUBY. Projective energy, men, compassion, force, movement, aggression, male sexuality, father.

5. THE CHIEF - TOPAZ. Authority, captivity, confinement, abandonment, advice, employer, honor, technology.

6. THE LOVERS - ROSE QUARTZ. Love, sexuality, relationships, friendship, duality, polarity, symbiosis, balance, beauty, family.

7. THE ELEMENTS - STAUROLITE, CROSS STONE, ANY TWINNED CRYSTALS. Earth power, nature, self-control, triumph, success.

8. STRENGTH - DIAMOND, HERKIMER DIAMOND, GARNET. Power, courage, will power, activity.

9. THE WISE ELDER - SAPPHIRE, BLUE TOURMALINE. Wisdom, knowledge, mysticism, enlightenment.

10. THE SPIRAL - SARDONYX, BLACK OPAL. Transformation, fortune, luck, exterior energies, unknown factors.

11. JUSTICE - CARNELIAN. Law, legal matters, dominance, submission, outside authority.

12. INITIATION - BERYL, AQUAMARINE. Introspection, trials, tests, sacrifice.

13. CHANGE - AMBER. Renewal, beginnings, endings, health matters, trials.

14. TEMPERANCE - AMETHYST. Moderation, scattering of energies, nonfocused, closed, disciplined, balance.

15. FOLLY - BLACK DIAMOND, BLACK TOURMALINE, ANY SQUARE BLACK STONE. Addiction, delusion, pity, depression, violence, pettiness, lack of vision, control by others, submission.

16. FORCE - LODESTONE, LAVA. Adversity, accident, challenge, oppression.

17. THE STAR - METEORITE, ANY STAR STONE. Universal energies, astrology, eclipse, travel, hope.

18. THE MOON - MOONSTONE, CHALCEDONY. Psychism, emotions, depression, night, winter, sleep, dreams, tides, magnetism, water.

19. THE SUN - TIGER'S-EYE, SUNSTONE. Mental activity, overintellectualism, thought, visualization, contentment, employment, day, summer, the seasons.

20. REBIRTH - FOSSIL. Reversal, outcome, evolution, growth, life, childbirth, lessons.

21. THE UNIVERSE - OPAL, KUNZITE. Interplay, success, movement, harvest, overview, ability, completion, higher forces.

Admittedly, these are rather cryptic descriptions. In performing any type of divination, the diviner must interpret the symbols, as explained in the last chapter.

The simplest way to consult this stone tarot is to visualize your question, or the area in which you feel you need help.

While visualizing, reach into your bag of stones and draw one out. If you're in tune, if you've familiarized yourself with the stones and hold their meanings in mind, all you may need to do is look at the stone and say, "Yes. Of course."

Say I was wondering if a project I was considering—a new book, for example—would be worth the time and energy I'd invest in it. I call my publisher and talk to him about it, and I grill my friends for their responses to it, but I'm still unsure.

Then, I reach into my tarot bag and draw out a stone. Remember,

I'm not consciously trying to select any particular stone. Even if I can differentiate between the stones with my fingers, which is often the case, I simply allow my subconscious mind to choose the stone.

Feeling its energies in my hand, I look down and see an opal. *Opal—The Universe*. Success, movement and completion are the meanings which first come to mind. Harvest and ability are also involved here. It seems that the book will be a success.

If, when doing this, you feel the first stone hasn't given you the complete picture, choose another and interpret them together.

There are more complicated methods of consulting the stone tarot. These are called 'layouts'. Here several stones are chosen and placed on some flat surface in a particular pattern. The stones are then 'read' in conjunction with this pattern, in the proper order, and with the other nearby stones in mind.

There are endless variations of patterns which you can use. Here are two of them; feel free to make up your own.

THREE STONES

This is ideal for discerning the true nature of a problem, or for a general look at your life.

Place one stone slightly to the left of you. This represents the recent past that is influencing your current situation.

Place the second stone to the right of the first. This represents your current situation.

The third stone is placed to the right of the second and signifies the future.

Read all three stones together.

THE PENTAGRAM

The stones are laid out to form a rough pentagram or pentagon (five-sided) figure. Draw a five-pointed star with one point upward and lay the stones on this.

Place the first stone on the upper right point. This represents the emotions involved in the problem—your own and those of others.

Place the second stone on the lower right point. This represents conflict, binding and illusions which you may not be aware of. It can also represent the obstacles which must be faced.

The third stone is placed on the lower left-hand point. It represents the foundation of the problem, the basis for its existence, the forces at work behind it.

Place the fourth stone on the upper left-hand point. This stone symbolizes your thoughts on the subject at the current time. These thoughts may hinder or help you.

The fifth stone is placed on the top point and signifies the final outcome.

Read the stones in the order in which you placed them on the pentagram. You can lay down all five before starting to interpret them, or work with each one singly.

Remember to judge each stone in connection with the other nearby stones.

Of necessity this is merely an introduction to stone tarot divination. This is truly an area where those who work with it can evolve a unique, personal system.

If it speaks to you, use it. If you don't like my version of associating stones with the tarot, change it. Work with it every day, and you'll discover how fascinating and correct the stone tarot can be.

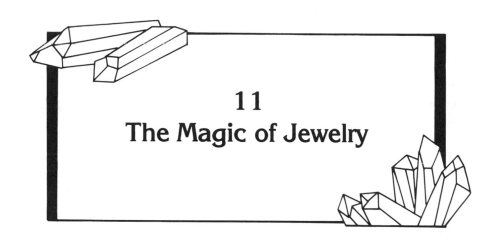

11
The Magic of Jewelry

Jewelry's origins lie in magic. That should come as no surprise to us, for as I've said, nearly all human customs and the technologies which result from those customs stem from ancient magical practices and beliefs.

In the earliest times, jewelry was probably worn to avert negativity, then envisioned as "evil spirits." Jewelry was also often placed in tombs with other grave goods to guard the dead.

As perception of the energies within objects sharpened, certain stones and metals were associated with various organs and regions of the body and were worn to guard the health. Later, stones, metals, horn, feathers, bone and many other materials were donned for their power to attract love, health, money and other necessities of life.

At first, humans recognized the energies within natural products of the earth and utilized these in their rites. When mining, metallurgy and lapidary became more sophisticated, artificially created pieces began to be used in magic.

Where materialism has ruled over naturalism, jewelry has survived purely as ornamentation or, at times, as a statement of class definition. Yes, jewelry still has a few ceremonial roles, such as engagement and wedding bands, but even these have lost their original magical messages.

This chapter is a brief look at the powers and symbolism of

jewelry, past and present. Until the nineteenth century in much of the Western world, the history of jewelry was a history of magic, so old books contain a wealth of information on this fascinating subject. Those who wish to further explore jewelry magic can consult the Bibliography for suggested works.

RINGS

The ring is a circle, symbolic of eternity, unity, reincarnation and the universe. In earlier times the ring was associated with the Sun and Moon. It was an object of protection, a magical guard that warded off negativity through its continuity.

Rings are still an accepted symbol of marriages and other unions because of their association with eternity.

All rings were once magical or sacred. Even goddesses and gods wore rings; Babylonian mythology is replete with stories of the rings of Shamash and Marduk. Rings have also been linked to the zodiac, the yin/yang and the 'magic circle' of magicians and Wiccans. Their magical history is complex and fascinating.

In a magical sense, wearing a ring 'binds' you with power, with energy. The materials of which the ring is constructed, plus your visualization, determine the nature of this energy.

The binding symbolism of the ring was so omnipresent and accepted that rings were soon subjected to religious and magical restrictions. Priests of various deities in ancient Greece and Rome removed their rings prior to entering sacred space. Some were eternally forbidden to wear them. During a trip to an oracle in ancient times, no flesh was eaten, sex was avoided, and rings were not worn. Even today, some shamans remove all knots and rings from their bodies prior to magical ritual.

Because rings kept energies in the body, they were also thought to inhibit the release of power. In any type of magical operation in which personal power is sent towards the magical need, rings were taboo because of the belief that they would lessen the effectiveness of the magic.

In spiritual rituals, in which we open ourselves to higher beings, rings were thought to block this process due, once again, to their restricting quality.

The appearance or attractiveness of a ring, and certainly its material value, are of little importance in magic. The ring's design, the metals and stones used are the only factors involved in selecting rings for magic.

Today, magical rings can be purchased from occult stores or sometimes made-to-order for specific ritual purposes. Better still, many practitioners are creating their own through the craft of the lapidary.

The finger on which a ring is worn has magical significance. The index or "ring" finger was once thought to be especially powerful. Herbal medicines were applied to the body with the ring finger to strengthen the effectiveness of the cure. Thus, rings containing stones which speed the body's healing are best worn on this finger.

The second or middle finger, which, upraised, is used as the ultimate gesture of insult in the United States, has long been thought to be an unlucky finger on which to wear rings.

Once, rings were usually worn on the third finger, because it was thought to contain a nerve that went directly to the heart. Betrothal rings are still traditionally worn on this finger.

NECKLACES

The necklace is simply a large ring worn around the neck. Its powers and uses are much the same as those of rings. Because necklaces are often worn near the heart, they can be used to work on the emotions, or to attract or strengthen love.

In contemporary Wicca, women often wear necklaces of stones to represent reincarnation and the Goddess.

Wearing a necklace of stones increases their energies because you are surrounding yourself (binding yourself) with their powers. Thus, the necklace is much more powerful than any one stone used separately.

EARRINGS

Earrings were once worn to guard the ears from negativity and disease. Later they became a symbol of slavery, for slaves wore earrings marking their status.

Earrings are rings that are worn in the ears. Piercing the lobes to allow the wearing of earrings is an ancient practice.

Most parts of the body have been pierced for various magical and religious reasons throughout the ages. Ears may have been among the first, along with the nose which is still pierced in India for protective, as well as cosmetic reasons.

Folklore still surrounds this practice. Pierced earrings in general are often recommended to strengthen weak eyes—if set with emeralds, they are particularly effective. Gold earrings are often worn by those wishing to cure headaches, though some say to wear one gold earring and one silver for this purpose.

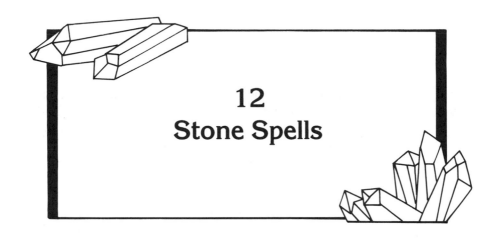

12
Stone Spells

Just as semiprecious and precious stones have been used for a wide variety of magical purposes, so too have plain, ordinary stones. Nothing in nature is without its magical uses.

In the preceding chapters, we've looked at how color, form, appearance, clarity and other factors help us know the powers within stones. In Part II of this book, you'll find detailed articles discussing the major magical stones.

This chapter is somewhat different. It contains minor rituals utilizing any kind of stone you find in your backyard, on the beach or anywhere out in nature.

In these spells, use your powers of visualization and concentration to direct the energy through the stones. Here, the rocks are usually focal points or tools that add little power of their own. Some of them are amulets and talismans of a kind. The stone pile, detailed below under 'Cairn of Power', collects energies from the earth, but the rocks themselves aren't necessarily powerful.

That's not to say that a piece of granite made up of quartz, hornblende and various other minerals doesn't contain its own powers, but such stones lack focused energy. Since this is the kind most needed in magic, it is more difficult to work with them than with amethyst and carnelian. Therefore, in the simple spells that follow, don't worry about which stone to use. Take whatever is at hand.

PROTECTION

The Five Pebbles

Go to a moving brook or stream. While standing in the water and facing downstream, remove five small pebbles from the streambed. As you do this, visualize your need for protection.

As your hand closes over the pebbles, see them beaming out protective energies. Just as the pebbles are hard and have weathered for eons, so too will they strengthen your protective shield.

Now carry them at all times for protection. If you wish, place them in a small pouch or a fold of cloth, or incorporate them into some form of jewelry.

Crossing a River

If you must cross a dangerous or unknown river and wish to have extra security on your side, stand before it. Bend and pick up three *dry* pebbles from the ground.

Carry these with you as you cross, visualizing yourself standing on the other side, wet but safe.

Once arriving there without mishap, place them back on the ground. It is done.

Protection at Night

If you feel danger is near when walking among trees at night, fortify yourself by picking up a small stone. Hold it in your projective hand and visualize yourself as *being* the stone—strong, hardy, protected.

Once your visualization is complete, throw the stone at the foot of a tree. You are protected.

DIVINATION

The Well

On a still night, take a large, round stone to a well. Still your mind and focus your awareness on the area of inquiry.

Then let the stone drop into the water. Listen to the sound the water makes as it strikes the water—in the water's sounds, you may hear answers to your questions. If not, perform this ritual again and let the splash speak to your subconscious mind.

Black and White

Spend a few minutes gathering stones. Half should be dark and half of a lighter color.

Place them on the ground before you. Ask your question or keep it in mind. Close your eyes and jumble the stones around for a few seconds; then, with your left or receptive hand, remove one of the stones.

If you picked a dark stone, the answer is yes or the prospects favorable. If light, no.

MONEY AND PROSPERITY

New Year's Stone

At sunrise on the morning of the new year, go outside and find the largest stone you can carry. Take this back to your house and put it in a place of prominence.

If you keep the stone in your house for a year, it will be one filled with prosperity. Replace the stone every year.

LUCK

On the Fence

Rise before the Sun on the morning of the Spring Equinox. Find several stones and place these on the fenceposts that surround your property, visualizing yourself, your home and life filled with luck.

It will be so.

LOVE

Stone Love

Go to a place that contains many water-worn stones. Look for a large, flat rock while visualizing yourself being involved with the perfect mate.

On this rock, mark with red ink two intertwined hearts. As you do this, keep the visualization in mind.

When you are finished, bury the stone in the earth in an uncultivated place.

POWER

Cairn of Power

This spell is ideal for use during outdoor rituals. Perform it prior to any other form of stone magic.

For additional power during spells, select ten or twenty small, round stones of approximately the same size. On the ground near where you'll perform magic, place the first stone. Say something like:

A stone of power.

Repeat this with the rest of the stones, gradually forming a triangular-shaped pile of stones. You are fashioning a cairn.

As you place the last stone on top of the pile, say words such as these:

A cairn of power.

Now perform any magic. Such cairns or stone piles seem to be collectors and reservoirs of power, and can help your magic.

They can also be permanently placed inside your home or, with larger cairns, outside on your property for protection.

A STONE-ATTRACTION SPELL

Take any stone. Hold it in your projective hand for several minutes while visualizing your need.

Flood the stone with your need and with your emotional involvement with your need. Send power out from your body to the stone. Use your visualization to see it streaming into the rock.

Then throw the stone into running water. It is done.

A STONE-BANISHING SPELL

To be rid of diseases, unhealthy habits, hurt feelings and any other disturbing manifestations of life, hold any stone in your projective hand and visualize the problem in detail.

Visualize the part of you that is to be banished as entering the stone. See the problem and its causes leaving you and infusing the stone.

When you can send no more energy into it, throw the stone onto a hot fire, throwing with it the causes and manifestations of your problem. Stand back—the stone may explode.

If you have no fire or don't wish to have rocks exploding, throw the stone into the air or into water, thereby releasing the problem-causing energy from your body.

It is done.

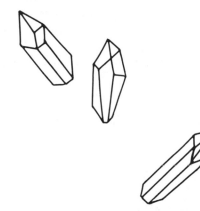

PART II
MAGIC AND LORE

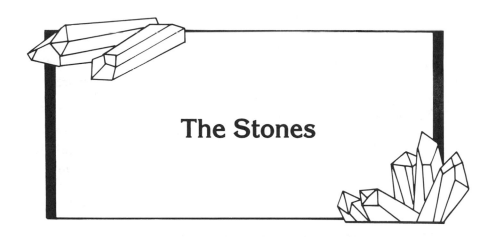

The Stones

This, the main section of this book, consists of alphabetically arranged listings of well over one hundred stones and minerals. There are articles covering seventy-eight major stones, some of which contain shorter discussions of several others.

In presenting this information, I've used the same format as that in *Cunningham's Encyclopedia of Magical Herbs*. It is compact, convenient and yet comprehensive.

First, I've listed the *common name*; at least, one of the most common names for the stone. If you know a stone by a different name than the common one I've used here, check the Index for help in locating the stone.

Following this are other common names by which the stone is known, here termed *folk names*.

The stone's basic *energy type*, projective or receptive, is next.

Planetary and *elemental attributions* follow. (For more information regarding the magical workings of the planets, see Part IV.)

Next, any *deities* associated with the stone are listed, followed by *metals* and *herbs* which are in some way connected with it.

The stone's basic *powers*, *magical/ritual lore* and *magical uses* complete each article.

Not all articles contain all of this information.

I hope it's understood that some of this information is subjective.

Endless discussions could occur over the "proper" planet to which quartz crystal should be assigned. Some of the stones only recently used in magic, such as lepidolite and kunzite, present challenges in assigning them to the elements and the planets.

The associations here are only suggestions.

I've used this basic format for most of the stones, but there are exceptions. For example, agate, immediately below, is found in numerous colors, each with its own traditional energies. Thus, this information will be found within the body of the article.

Part II can be read straight through or used for reference as you discover new stones.

May the power of stones enrich your life.

AGATE

Folk Names: Red Agate, Blood Agate
Energy: various (see below)
Planet: Mercury (generally speaking)
Element: various (see below)
Deity: Aesculapius
Powers: Strength, Courage, Longevity, Gardening, Love, Healing, Protection
Magical Uses:

In general, the agate is utilized in spells and magical rituals involving strength, bravery, longevity and so on.

Worn on the arm or carried while gardening, the agate increases your plants' fertility and ensures a bountiful crop or healthy flowers. Moss agate (see below) was thought to be the best suited for this. Charged agates can be 'planted' in the garden to promote abundance, and small agates hung on trees increase their yield.

In ancient Rome an agate worn in a ring on the hand or bound to the left arm ensured the favor of the vegetative deities, who would cause the Earth to be fruitful.

A stone often utilized in love spells, agate is also worn to avoid envious thoughts and to remove spite; in other words, to make its wearer amiable and agreeable. Spite has no place in the search for love.

It is also worn as a truth amulet, to ensure that your words are pure, and also to ensure favors from powerful persons.

Agate jewelry is given to children to be worn as protective

amulets. Agate is thought to be particularly useful in preventing children from falling and is also worn by adults to avoid stumbling.

An agate held in the mouth relieves thirst. It was once used to reduce fevers by applying it to the forehead. Held in the hand the agate calms and refreshes the body and helps it heal minor health problems

Agates were popular talismans in the Middle East to ensure the healthy state of the blood. In ancient Britain they were worn to guard against skin diseases. Triangular-shaped agates were used in Syria to avert intestinal problems.

In ceremonial magic, agates were engraved with serpents or men riding on snakes. Worn as an amulet this magical jewel prevented snake, scorpion and insect bites and stings.

The agate is sometimes used in protective spells and rituals and was once thought to be a sovereign guard against sorcery, demons and fiendish possession.

In Asia, agates were used much as quartz crystal is today. To ascertain future trends the scryer gazed at the markings on the stone, allowing the deep mind to project its psychic impulses to the conscious mind.

The numerous types of agate—vaguely distinguishable by color or markings—are used in various types of magic. Though any type of agate may be worn for the above uses, these particular stones have traditional energies. Here's a list of some of the major ones and their magical attributions:

Banded Agate: (Energy: Projective, Element: Fire) Protection. Restores bodily energy and eases stressful situations.

Black Agate: (Energy: Projective, Element: Fire) Another protective stone. Wear for courage and successful competitions.

Black and White Agate: (Energy: Receptive, Element: Earth) Worn as an amulet, this stone guards against physical dangers.

Blue Lace Agate: (Energy: Receptive, Element: Water) Wear or carry for peace and happiness. Place in your hand to de-stress. Lay one on your desk or other work station and gaze at it when in stressful situations. In the home, a blue lace agate surrounded with flaming, light blue candles calms the psychic atmosphere and reduces household or family quarrels.

Brown or Tawny Agate: (Energy: Projective, Element: Fire) Once worn by warriors for victory in battle, the brown agate is used today for success in any undertaking. It was prized in Italy and Persia as a guard against the evil eye. It's also a wealth talisman.

Green Agate: (Energy: Receptive, Element: Earth) Worn to improve the health of the eyes. In the past, a woman who drank the water a green agate ring was washed in was magically guarded against sterility.

Moss Agate: (Energy: Receptive, Element: Earth) Due to its curious markings, which suggest moss or trees, the moss agate is the especial gardener's talisman. It is worn to relieve a stiff neck, to lend energy to the depleted, and for healing purposes. It is also used in spells involving riches, happiness and long life. Wear this stone to make new friends and to discover "treasure."

Red Agate: (Energy: Projective, Element: Fire) Also known as "Blood Agate," this stone was worn in ancient Rome to guard against insect bites, to heal the blood, and to promote calm and peace.

ALEXANDRITE
Powers: Luck, Love
Magical Uses:

This gemstone is rare and expensive. When worn, alexandrite draws luck and good fortune. It is also used in love spells.

ALUM
Energy: Receptive
Planet: Saturn
Element: Earth
Powers: Protection
Magical Uses:

Alum has been worn in Egypt as a protective amulet against evil. On the north coast of Africa, alum is also used for this purpose. A piece of alum is placed in the home to guard it, and small amounts of this mineral are sewn into or placed in children's hats to protect them as well.

AMAZONITE
Folk Name: Amazon Stone
Energy: Receptive
Planet: Uranus
Element: Earth
Powers: Gambling, Success

Magical Uses:

This bluish green feldspar is worn by gamblers to attract money luck. It is also used by anyone taking a chance to ensure success.

AMBER

Energy: Projective
Planet: Sun
Elements: Fire, Akasha
Deity: The Great Mother
Powers: Luck, Healing, Strength, Protection, Beauty, Love
Magical/Ritual Lore:

Amber is perhaps the oldest substance used for human adornment. Beads and pendants of amber have been found in northern European gravesites dating back to 8000 B.C.E. (before the common era; the nonreligious equivalent of B.C.)

It is not a stone, but fossilized resin of coniferous (cone-bearing, like modern pine) trees of the Oligocene epoch. It often contains fragments or complete specimens of insects and plants that accidentally fell into the sticky resin millions of years ago.

Because amber, unlike gemstones, is warm to the touch and often contains insect fragments, it was thought to possess life. The early Chinese visualized the souls of tigers transmuting into amber upon their earthly deaths. It was sacred to worshippers of the Mother Goddess in classical times because it was believed to contain the very essence of life itself—the animating principle.

Because amber is a fossil, it has associations with time, cycles and longevity. Similarly, since it was once a living substance, it is related to Akasha. This is the 'fifth element', which governs and binds together Earth, Air, Fire and Water, and, in a sense, is the ultimate source of them. Akasha is also symbolic of life and living things (plants, animals, humans).

In some contemporary Wiccan covens women—usually High Priestesses—wear necklaces consisting of alternating amber and jet beads. Though reasons for the use of these materials vary, it is said that these two stones represent the Goddess and God, the feminine and masculine principles, the projective and receptive forces of nature. They also heighten magical effects.

Amber rubbed against wool or silk becomes electrically charged. Its old Greek name was *elektron*, from which we derive our modern word *electricity*.

All these mysterious properties and associations make amber one of the most widely used and prized magical substances of all times and places on Earth.

Magical Uses:

Amber, in common with a few other stones, has been utilized for nearly every purpose in magic. It has figured in countless millions of spells and magical rituals.

Despite its high price amber is a sound magical investment. Just buy it from a reliable dealer—much that is sold as amber is glass, plastic or "reconstituted amber." Insist on genuine, unprocessed amber. And be prepared to pay quite a bit for it.

Amber necklaces are perhaps the commonest form utilized in magic. Such necklaces are protective when worn. It is a potent amulet against negative magic and is especially effective in safeguarding children. Have children wear amber beads to guard their health, as countless others have done in many parts of the world. Or place a bit in the child's bedroom.

In ancient times, when sex was viewed as a completely natural and yet sacred activity, representations of the generative organs were commonly used in magic. Amber carved in the shape of a phallus was carried as a supremely potent magical protectant. Though this seems to be the product of patriarchy, I'm sure that images of the female organs were just as effective, and used just as much, but this information has been suppressed.

If you feel you are being subjected to heavy negativity, light a white candle and place it on the ground or floor. Sit before it with a handful of small amber beads, and using them, create a circle around yourself. Sit within the circle while restoring your energy and closing yourself off to any and all outside influences. Repeat as necessary.

Another protective use of amber is to place nine small beads or pieces into a bath of very warm water. Soak in the tub until the water cools, then retrieve the amber, towel off, and carry or wear one of the beads until your next bath.

Witches, Wise Women, and shamans wear amber beads to strengthen their spells, whether cast in caves, deserted valleys or at lonely seashores, or within magically created spheres of power in urban bedrooms. A large piece of amber placed on the altar increases the effectiveness of your magic.

Amber is worn to enhance beauty and general attractiveness. During the Renaissance the donning of amber was said to increase bodily weight; however, this was probably because the buxom female figure was then in fashion. There's no evidence to support this claim. Amber does seem to magnify its wearer's natural beauty, attract friends and companions to the lonely, and stimulate happiness.

Amber has long been regarded as being highly sensual and magnetic. It is worn to attract love and to increase one's enjoyment of pleasurable activities, including sex. Small pieces of amber can be added to herbal love-attracting mixtures or worn near the heart to attract a mate.

Human fertility was a constant concern in past ages, and it still is for many. Women wore images of fish, frogs and rabbits carved of amber to ensure conception. To combat impotency and to ensure their own fertility, men wore amber figures of lions, dogs and dragons. This may seem quaint, but such images charged with magical energy and worn with ritual intent can work. There are no limitations in magic, save for those we impose upon ourselves.

In our quest to rid our bodies of disease, amber plays an important role. Beads of amber are worn around the neck as a general protector of health and to relieve or cure existing conditions. It has been worn for the prevention or relief of convulsions, deafness, insanity, sore throat, earache, headache, toothache, asthma, rheumatism, digestive troubles and almost every internal ailment. A ball of amber held in the hand reduces a fever.

Because it is often translucent, or even transparent, amber is worn or carried to strengthen the eyes. Looking through a piece of amber is thought to do the same.

Amber powder was burned during childbirth to assist the woman's labor and, also, was smouldered so the piney smoke could be sniffed to halt a nosebleed.

Amber's magical uses extend beyond the above information. It is worn to increase strength, utilized for business success or to stimulate the flow of money toward the magician, and plays a part in attraction spells. These include rituals designed to draw love, money, power and success. Finally, a bit of powdered amber added to any incense will increase its effectiveness.

AMETHYST
Energy: Receptive
Planets: Jupiter, Neptune
Element: Water

Deities: Bacchus, Dionysus, Diana
Powers: Dreams, Overcoming Alcoholism, Healing, Psychism, Peace,
Love, Protection Against Thieves, Courage, Happiness
Magical Uses:

Amethyst, a purple quartz, is a stone steeped in ancient magic. It is, perhaps, as popular today as it was two thousand years ago.

Placed beneath the pillow or worn to bed, amethyst drives off insomnia and nightmares. It produces a peaceful sleep and pleasant, healing, even prophetic dreams. However, it will also ensure that its wearer doesn't oversleep.

A spiritual stone, with absolutely no negative side effects or associations with violence, anger or passion, the amethyst is the stone of peace. When the stresses of everyday life well up within you, hold an amethyst in your left hand (or right hand if left-handed). Let its soothing, de-stressing, calming, peaceful vibrations sink into you. Or better yet, wear amethyst so that it touches your skin, and you may avoid such highly wrought emotional states.

The amethyst calms fears, raises hopes, lifts the spirits and promotes thoughts of the spiritual reality behind our lives. Worn, it wards off guilt and self-deception, helps you overcome addictions such as alcoholism, curbs overindulgence and bestows good judgment. Amethyst calms emotional storms. Even in situations of potential danger the amethyst will come to your aid.

Amethyst also lends courage to its wearer, and it is a powerful amulet for travelers. Worn, it protects against thieves, harm, sickness and danger.

In Renaissance magic, amethysts engraved with the image of a bear were worn as protective amulets. In Graeco-Roman times rings of amethyst set in bronze were worn as charms against evil, and magical cups carved from amethyst banished sorrow and evil from all who drank.

Because it is such a spiritual stone, the amethyst is often worn during contemplation or placed on simple meditation altars. A piece set before a white candle and a censer burning a soothing, high-vibrational incense, such as sandalwood, is conducive to meditative practices.

Pre-meditation baths can be powerful attunement experiences. Have a light purple candle burning as you bathe, and ring the candle with amethysts.

The amethyst is also used to increase psychic awareness and to sharpen the 'sixth sense'. Some keep an amethyst with their tarot cards, I Ching yarrow stalks or coins, or rune stones to heighten their inner energies. It is, naturally, worn during psychic or divinatory acts. Since it is also a stone of wisdom, it allows the information received through the psychic mind to be appropriately utilized.

This beautiful stone also sharpens the conscious mind, quickening the wit and enhancing mental powers. It is utilized to improve the memory, to relieve headaches and to keep thoughts in line with life goals.

A stone of pure, true emotional love, it is often exchanged between lovers to strengthen their commitment. An amethyst carved in the shape of a heart and set in silver was presented by a woman to a man to ensure their love.

Amethyst is also one of the few stones specifically prescribed for men to use for attracting women. Worn by a man, the stone draws "good women" to love him.

Though it is often thought to be a stone of chastity, this attribution dates from past centuries when the ideal love was 'platonic'. Today, when more and more persons view sex as a natural aspect of a healthy, monogamous relationship, this idea is slowly fading from folk memory.

The amethyst is used by those involved with lawsuits to ensure that right is done. It is also utilized in prosperity magic and has long been thought to bring success to businesses, perhaps because of its Jupiterian rulership.

Hundreds of years ago the amethyst was moistened with saliva and rubbed on the face to banish pimples and rough skin. Today it is used in spells designed to magnify beauty.

An amethyst spell: When emotionally upset, jilted by a lover, ending a relationship, stressed to the point of severe mental problems, or when in any unstable condition, go to a place outside where you can be alone. Hold an amethyst in your left hand (or right, if left-handed). *Pour* out all your feelings, your emotions, from your body through your arm, out your palm and into the stone.

Feel every pain, every emotional low, every hurt. Send it into the stone with all the force of your innate magical abilities.

When the stone is nearly bursting with negativity, throw it with as much force as you can muster. Scream, howl, choke out a shout as you throw the stone. As your hand releases the amethyst, *release the hurt as well. KNOW* that it is in the stone, that it is outside you, that it is now alien to you.

Calm down, breathe deeply, meditate for a few moments. Thank the Earth for its help, then turn around and leave your problems behind you.

The earth will absorb the hurt, leaving the stone free, but never bring that stone into your life again.

APACHE TEAR
Energy: Projective
Planet: Saturn
Element: Fire
Powers: Protection, Luck
Magical Uses:

The Apache tear, a globule of translucent obsidian, is carried as a good-luck charm. It is also used for protective purposes as well as all of those ascribed to obsidian.

AQUAMARINE
Energy: Receptive
Planet: Moon
Element: Water
Powers: Psychism, Peace, Courage, Purification
Magical/Ritual Lore:

The aquamarine is the stone of the sea-goddesses of past times. Beads of aquamarine were found in ancient Egyptian mummy pits.
Magical Uses:

The aquamarine, a semiprecious variety of beryl, is a pale blue-green color and so has long been associated with the sea and with the element of Water. Sea Witches cleanse the stone in ocean water at night by the light of the Full Moon. To do the same far from the coast, fill a blue vessel with water, add sea salt and let the stone sit in this mixture overnight.

In magic this beautiful stone is worn or carried to enhance the utilization of psychic powers. Holding a crystal of the stone, or wearing a faceted aquamarine around the neck reduces our conscious mind's hold on the psychic mind and allows the ever-present psychic impulses to be heard and to enter our consciousness.

Because the aquamarine is a cleansing and purificatory stone, it can be worn or rubbed on the body as a part of a purification prior to magical acts. A large crystal can also be worn or placed in the bathtub during cleansing dips.

A gentle cleansing tincture can be made by placing an aquamarine in a glass of fresh water. Let this sit in full moonlight, outdoors if possible, for three hours. Retrieve the stone and drink the liquid for purification and heightened psychic awareness.

Aquamarine is used much like the amethyst in soothing and calming emotional problems. It is a stone of peace, joy and happiness, especially in relationships. Aquamarines exchanged by mates help smooth the path of their interactions, and it is a most magically appropriate gift for a bridegroom to give his bride on the day of their nuptials.

Aquamarine is worn or carried as a protective amulet while sailing or flying over water. When packing for a trip on water, whether a river cruise or a journey across the Pacific Ocean, tuck an aquamarine in your suitcase to guard against storms. Fishermen and sailors have long made it their special amulet against danger.

Aquamarine has also been worn to relieve the pain of toothache and to cure illness of the stomach, throat and jaw.

As a charm the aquamarine is worn to ensure good health, to halt fear so as to strengthen the courage hiding behind it, and for alertness of the mind.

ASBESTOS
Energy: Projective
Planet: Mars
Element: Fire
Power: Protection
Magical/Ritual Lore:

In the past asbestos was viewed as a magical stone since it can be continuously burned without being consumed. It was used to make wicks for the perpetual fires in ancient Greek temples.
Magical Uses:

Surprisingly, asbestos is nothing more than a mass of flexible, perfect prismatic crystals, usually a variety of serpentine or crocidolite. When associated with quartz and polished, it is known as tiger's-eye.

The irresponsible use of asbestos in manufacturing and housing has caused countless illnesses today. In the past, however, long before it was misused, asbestos was worn for protection against negative magic and the evil eye, which was thought to be a form of intentional or nonintentional psychic attack.

Asbestos is no longer recommended for magical use.

AVENTURINE
Energy: Projective
Planet: Mercury
Element: Air
Powers: Mental Powers, Eyesight, Gambling, Money, Peace, Healing, Luck
Magical Uses:

Green aventurine is worn to strengthen the eyesight. It is also worn, carried or used in spells designed to increase perception, to stimulate creativity and to enhance intelligence.

This stone is utilized in games of chance magic and is a popular gambler's talisman. Aventurine is also used in money-attracting magic.

Its green color tells us of its usefulness in calming troubled emotions and in speeding healing.

Aventurine is an all-around luck stone.

AZURITE
Folk Names: *Lapis Linguis, Lapis Lingua*
Energy: Receptive
Planet: Venus
Element: Water
Powers: Psychism, Dreams, Divination, Healing
Magical Uses:

Azurite, a beautiful, deep blue stone, has long been utilized in magic to increase psychic powers. Place the stone beneath the pillow for prophetic dreams. Hold or wear an azurite when divining the future.

A simple divinatory spell: Place a piece of azurite between two white candles in a darkened room. Light the candles. Hold the azurite in your hand until it is warm, emptying your mind of thought.

Close your eyes until you feel the azurite's soft, slow energies touching your hand. Then open your eyes and gaze at the stone until answers or messages come through.

Azurite is also used in healing magic.

BERYL
Energy: Receptive

Planet: Moon
Element: Water
Deities: Poseidon, Neptune, Tiamat, Mara
Associated Herbs: Seaweed (any type)
Powers: Psychism, Healing, Love, Energy, Anti-Gossip
Magical/Ritual Lore:

In fifth-century Ireland, scryers who used beryl spheres were known as *specularii*. Dr. Dee's famous crystal, now housed in the British Museum, was of beryl, not clear quartz crystal as is often imagined. Ancient peoples utilized the beryl in rituals designed to bring rain.

Magical Uses:

Another stone related to the sea, like the aquamarine, beryl is worn while on the water for protection against storms. This stone guards its wearer against drowning and also, prosaically enough, seasickness.

It is worn to prevent fascination, or what would today be called deliberate psychic manipulation or persuasion, such as is practiced by evangelists, some salespersons and politicians. In this sense it is also carried to make its bearer unconquerable and to assuage fear, increase optimism and happiness.

In the 16th century, magicians prescribed beryl to be worn to win all debates and arguments, and yet to cause its bearer to be well mannered and amiable, and to gain understanding.

Beryl has long been used to increase psychic awareness. As such, it was called the stone of the seer. Spheres of beryl were at one time considered to be superior to those of quartz crystal. It was also carved into flat, round mirrors for scrying purposes. These, like the spheres, were sometimes held in white cloth and gazed at while the conscious mind drowsed.

According to ancient magical directions, beryl-scrying should be practiced only during the waxing Moon for the most potent results. Because of its associations with lunar energy, beryl can be worn or placed on the altar during Full Moon rituals.

When you have lost something, hold a beryl in your hand and visualize the object. Then still your mind and let your psychic impressions reveal its whereabouts.

It is another stone exchanged between lovers to strengthen their relationship and is carried or worn to attract love.

The beryl is also used to send energy into the body as well as to halt gossip. During study, wear beryl to increase your conscious mind's retention of information.

In the 13th century an image of a frog was engraved on beryl, and the stone was carried to reconcile enemies and to attract friendship.

For healing purposes the beryl was considered to be excellent in relieving liver ailments, swollen glands and diseases of the eyes.

If you feel lazy, hold or wear a beryl and let its structured, low vibrations enter you.

BLOODSTONE
Folk Names: Heliotrope, Hematite (which is a different stone)
Energy: Projective
Planet: Mars
Element: Fire
Associated Herb: Heliotrope (*Heliotropum europaeum*)
Powers: Halting Bleeding, Healing, Victory, Courage, Wealth, Strength, Power, Legal Matters, Business, Invisibility, Agriculture
Magical/Ritual Lore:

Bloodstone, a green chalcedony flecked with red spots, has been used in magic for at least three thousand years. In ancient Babylon the stone was carried to overcome enemies and was used in ancient Egypt to open doors, break bonds and even cause stone walls to fall.

Its most famous use is to halt bleeding. It was frequently carried by soldiers to either avoid wounds or as a magical first aid. When pressed on wounds, the stone caused the bleeding to stop. Though this was considered to be pure magic, the effect was probably due to the pressure and the cool temperature of the stone. Today it is still worn to keep the blood healthy and to help cure blood-related diseases. A bloodstone held to the nose is said to 'lock' it, i.e., to stop the flow of blood.

It was also worn to cure fevers and as a general health-giving talisman.
Magical Uses:

Because of its associations with blood, it is a popular stone with athletes. They wear it to increase physical strength and to win competitions. It is also worn to lengthen the life span.

The bloodstone which is worn lends courage, calms fears and eliminates anger. It has long been used in spells designed to secure victory in court and legal matters.

Because it is green, it is utilized in wealth, money and business spells. A bloodstone kept in the cash register draws money. Carried in the pocket or purse, or worn, it also attracts wealth. In this regard, since food and money are magically connected, it was a farmer's talisman in the Middle Ages, worn during planting to increase the yield of crops.

Women hung a bloodstone on the arm to prevent miscarriage and, later, on the thigh to ease childbirth.

For invisibility, the bloodstone was smeared with fresh heliotrope flowers and worn or carried. This was said to dazzle the eyes of the bearer's beholders. Today this ritual may be used for 'magical invisibility'—when you wish to lay low and not attract attention to yourself.

In the 13th century, bloodstones were engraved with the figure of a bat. These talismans were worn by magicians to increase the effectiveness of spells and magical rites.

CALCITE
Folk Name: Iceland Spar
Energy: various (see below)
Planet: various (see below)
Element: various (see below)
Powers: Spirituality, Centering, Peace, Love, Healing, Purification, Money, Protection, Energy
Magical Uses:

Calcite, a transparent crystal, is found in a wide variety of colors, including clear, green, pink, orange and blue.

Calcite has the unique optical quality of double refraction. Draw a line with a pen on a piece of paper, then place a piece of calcite over the line. When you look through the stone, the line will appear to be doubled.

This property causes calcite to be used in spells to 'double the power' of the rite. It is placed on the altar or worn during magical ritual for this purpose.

Clear Calcite: (Energy: Receptive, Planet: Moon, Element: Water) This stone is utilized in spirituality rituals. It is perfect as a focus of contemplation during meditation.

Pink Calcite: (Energy: Receptive, Planet: Venus, Element: Water) Held in the hand, pink calcite is calming, centering and grounding. It is also used in love rituals.

Blue Calcite: (Energy: Receptive, Planet: Venus, Element: Water)

Blue calcite is a healing stone when worn on the body, or placed between flaming purple or blue candles. During purification ceremonies, wear or use blue calcite.

Green Calcite: (Energy: Receptive, Planet: Venus, Element: Earth) This stone draws money and prosperity to the household, especially when surrounded by flaming green candles every morning for a few minutes.

Orange Calcite: (Energy: Projective, Planet: Sun, Element: Fire) Orange Calcite is a protective stone and lends energy to the body when held.

CARNELIAN
Energy: Projective
Planet: Sun
Element: Fire
Powers: Protection, Peace, Eloquence, Healing, Courage, Sexual
 Energy
Magical Uses:

Carnelian, a red form of chalcedony, was worn on the hand in ancient Egypt to still anger, jealousy, envy and hatred. It is still used to promote peace and harmony and to dispel depression.

The stone is worn by the shy and timid to bolster their courage. It is an excellent stone to wear or carry for public speaking, one of the most common fears in today's world. The carnelian strengthens the voice, provides self-confidence and confers eloquence on the speaker. It is usually worn on the neck or in a ring for these purposes.

Carnelian is also used to counteract doubt and negative thoughts, and can be utilized in spells relating to these problems. It also confers patience.

Carnelian is carried to guard against others who try to read your thoughts. In Renaissance magic the carnelian was engraved with a sword, or an image of a warrior. Then, this magical amulet was placed in the home to guard it from lightning and storms, and carried as a protectant against enchantments.

Carnelian was worn to prevent skin diseases, insanity, nosebleeds and all blood diseases, and as a general health-inducer.

The carnelian strengthens astral vision and is worn to bed to halt nightmares.

This stone is also worn to stimulate sexual impulses.

CAT'S-EYE
Energy: Projective
Planet: Venus
Element: Earth
Powers: Wealth, Beauty, Gambling, Protection, Healing
Magical Uses:

Cat's-eye is a name applied to several different stones, usually a quartz containing olive-green asbestos. The ancient Asian cat's-eye, however, was a form of chrysoberyl.

This stone, which exhibits a moving luminous opalescence, is a beauty aid. It is worn or carried to increase beauty and to preserve youthfulness. A beauty tincture can be made by filling a green glass jar with fresh spring water, adding a cat's-eye, and leaving this in the Sun for three to six hours. Afterward, remove the stone. Wash your face with the water every day until it's gone and wear the stone.

Cat's-eye is also utilized in wealth and money spells. Possession of the stone guards the owner's wealth and will increase it as long as the stone is retained. It is often kept with money for this purpose. Not only does the stone prevent financial ruin, it will also restore wealth lost prior to ownership of the stone. Cat's-eye brings riches and is an excellent talisman for gamblers.

Cat's-eye set in a silver ring can be worn for mental health, protection, insight and luck. The stone also dispels depression, gives pleasure, and should be worn during financial speculation.

Because of its eyelike appearance, this stone is worn to help with diseases of the eyes.

A cat's-eye money spell: Take a bill of the highest denomination you have. Rub it completely with the cat's-eye, then tightly wrap the bill around the stone. Tie the bill firmly to it with green thread and carry in your pocket to increase your money. Don't spend the bill until the spell has worked.

The Assyrians believed the cat's-eye caused invisibility, probably because of the stone's dazzling appearance.

CELESTITE
Energy: Receptive
Planets: Venus, Neptune
Element: Water
Powers: Compassion, Eloquence, Healing

Magical Uses:

Celestite is worn or carried to create eloquence and to promote compassion for the Earth and our fellow creatures.

It is also used to relieve headaches and tension in the body, for it removes stress from the physical form.

CHALCEDONY

Energy: Receptive
Planet: Moon
Element: Water
Powers: Peace, Anti-Nightmare, Travel, Protection, Lactation, Luck
Magical Uses:

Chalcedony, in common with many other stones, banishes fear, hysteria, depression, mental illness and sadness. It also promotes calm and peaceful feelings when worn or held in the hand.

In the 16th century it was prescribed by magicians to dissolve illusions and fantasies. For this purpose it was pierced and hung around the neck.

Worn to bed or placed beneath the pillow, chalcedony drives away nightmares, night visions and fear of the dark.

As a protective stone, chalcedony guards its bearer during times of political revolution and while traveling. It is also used to ward off psychic attack and negative magic. Chalcedony prevents accidents if worn.

In Renaissance magic the chalcedony was engraved with the figure of a man with his right hand upraised. This was worn for success in lawsuits as well as for health and safety.

The stone is used for beauty, strength, energy and success in all undertakings, and in Italy, mothers wear beads of white chalcedony to increase lactation.

An arrowhead carved of chalcedony is worn or carried for luck.

CHRYSOCOLLA

Energy: Receptive
Planet: Venus
Element: Water
Powers: Peace, Wisdom, Love
Magical Uses:

Chrysocolla was once held in the hand to drive off unreasonable fear and illusions. It is a stone of peace and soothes the emotions.

When worn, the stone grants the power of discretion and increased wisdom.

Chrysocolla, a green stone, is also worn or utilized in spells to attract love. A simple love rite using this stone: At your stone altar, place a piece of chrysocolla in your hand. Visualize it attracting a love to you.

Place the stone in a small red or pink cup half-filled with water. In this, place three red roses.

Add fresh roses to the water as the others fade. Love will come into your life.

CHRYSOPRASE
Energy: Receptive
Planet: Venus
Element: Earth
Deity: Vesta
Powers: Happiness, Luck, Success, Friendship, Protection, Healing, Money
Magical Uses:

Chrysoprase, an apple-green form of chalcedony, is worn to lift the emotions and to banish greed, envy, selfishness, tension and stress. It is a cheering stone when worn, and is also used to prevent nightmares.

A lucky stone, chrysoprase is worn for eloquence, success in new undertakings, and to attract friends.

As a magical amulet of protection, in the 13th century the chrysoprase was engraved with the image of a bull and worn. Today it is utilized as a general shield against negativity.

Chrysoprase's healing powers include strengthening the eyes, staunching blood and relieving the pain of rheumatism.

To attract money, carry a small piece with you at all times.

CITRINE
Energy: Projective
Planet: Sun
Element: Fire
Powers: Anti-Nightmare, Protection, Psychism
Magical Uses:

Citrine is worn at night to remove fear, to prevent nightmares and to ensure a good night's sleep.

Citrine, a form of quartz, is also worn to facilitate psychic awareness.

COAL
Energy: Receptive
Planet: Saturn
Element: Earth
Power: Money
Magical Uses:

Coal, the common substance used to heat millions of homes, is considered by many to be an excellent money-attractant and hence is carried in the pocket and placed with money.

Speculators in the stock exchange in London often carry some coal with them for luck.

CORAL
Energy: Receptive
Planet: Venus
Elements: Water, Akasha
Deities: Isis, Venus, The Great Mother
Associated Metals: Silver, Copper
Powers: Healing, Regulating Menstruation, Agriculture, Protection, Peace, Wisdom
Magical/Ritual Lore:

Coral has played an important role in religious and magical rites throughout the Pacific Islands. It is often placed on graves to guard the deceased, and temples were sometimes built of lava rocks and coral.

In the Mediterranean, coral was thought, like amber, to contain the "life essence" of the Mother Goddess, who dwelled in the ocean in a "tree" of coral.

There is a Hindu belief that the ocean is the home of human souls after death, and so coral is considered a powerful amulet for the living. It is also placed on the body of the deceased to prevent 'evil spirits' from occupying it. In ancient Norse mythology coral is again linked with deity.

Because coral is neither a stone nor a plant substance, but the skeletal remains of a sea creature, many people object to its use in magic. We've gone beyond the time when we have to sacrifice living things (in this sense, coral) to practice magic.

However, I don't see how picking up a piece of coral that washed up on the beach in Florida, Hawaii or Italy harms anything. The commercial harvesting of living coral is another matter. It is up to you to decide if you wish to utilize commercial coral in magic.

Magical Uses:

On a warm, balmy day in Hawaii I walked along a deserted beach. The aquamarine waters glistened and gently lapped at the gritty coral sand. Then to my surprise and delight, a small piece of white coral washed up almost to my feet. A water-worn hole pierced the coral. I said my thanks and picked it up, recognizing it as a magical object.

In ancient times red coral was a gift from the deities. It was found on beaches throughout the world, but most often in Italy. To be powerful in magic, ancient people used coral which hadn't been worked by human hands; that is, it wasn't polished, ground, cut or carved. Because coral was thought to be alive (as it once was), people believed that any processing done to it would "kill" the magical energies within it. This isn't absolutely true today, but one belief is still current—if a piece of coral used in magic breaks for any reason, it has lost its power and a new piece must be obtained. Return the broken pieces to the ocean.

Coral comes from two Greek words meaning "daughter of the sea." Italian women used to wear it near the groin to regulate the menstrual flow, recognizing the link between coral, the sea, the Moon and their cycles. The coral, usually red, was believed to grow pale during the flow, then grow brighter afterward. It could have been used to predict their periods. Coral used for these purposes was carefully hidden from the eyes of men, for, if seen by them, it lost all its magic power.

Coral is still used in magic today. When worn so as to be plainly visible it is a protective amulet. It is used against "the evil eye, demons, furies, succubi, incubi and phantasma" among other ills. It guards against accidents, acts of violence, poison, theft, possession and sterility, the last especially in women.

Coral is also worn to effect inner changes. It dispels foolishness, nervousness, fear, depression, murderous thoughts, panic and nightmares. It confers reason, prudence, courage and wisdom upon its bearer. Placed beneath the pillow it produces peaceful sleep by driving away disturbing dreams.

Coral has been used in magic relating to children for thousands of years. If presented as a gift to a child, it ensures their future health.

Infants wear a coral pendant or beads to ease the pain of cutting teeth. It was also used in rattles to guard children. Place a piece of coral in a child's room to magically protect him or her.

A special use of coral was popular in ancient Egypt and Greece. Powdered coral was mixed with seed and sown or scattered over newly planted fields. This protected the growing crops from inclement weather and insects. Coral was also hung on fruit trees to increase their yield.

In healing, red coral was used to cure indigestion, all pains in the digestive tract, eye complaints and to staunch blood. Also, red coral when worn had the power to alert its wearer of ill health by paling in color.

Coral is used as a house luck-attractant. Take a piece of coral and touch it to every door, window and wall in the house while moving in a clockwise direction. Then put it in a place of prominence and let it do its magic.

It also has associations with love. Coral earrings were worn by women in ancient Rome to attract men. Powdered coral was used in 16th-century Venusian incenses, and red or pink candles ringed with pieces of coral are burned to draw love.

Because of its associations with the sea, coral is also worn as a protectant while sailing or traveling over water, and guards boats against shipwreck. It is also sometimes worn as protection against shark attack.

CROSS STONE
Folk Names: Cross-Stones, Fairy Crosses
Energies: Projective, Receptive
Powers: Elemental Magic, Elemental Power, Luck
Magical/Ritual Lore:
When a friend of mine returned from six months in northern California, she brought with her, among many other wonders, a piece of cross stone. Though she called it "fairy cross" (or fairy crosses), I recognized it as cross stone.

Shamans often include a piece of this stone in their medicine or power bags, and it is a favorite item to exchange with others during "giveaways."
Magical Uses:
The cross stone, apparently a form of andalusite, is found in coarse crystals. When these are broken open or sliced, they display a

symmetrical cross pattern of alternating light and dark colors.

Because of its shape, the cross stone is worn or carried by those practicing elemental magic or by those wishing to balance the four elements within themselves.

It is carried, worn, or placed on the altar for power during magical rituals of all kinds.

As with all stones exhibiting unusual shapes or patterns, it is carried for luck.

CRYSTAL, QUARTZ

Folk Names: Crystal, Witch's Mirror, Star Stone, Iris (from the prismatic effect of quartz crystals), *Zaztun* (Mayan)
Energies: Projective, Receptive
Planets: Sun, Moon
Elements: Fire, Water
Deity: The Great Mother
Associated Metals: Silver, Copper, Gold
Associated Herbs: Copal, Mugwort, Chicory, Sage, Sweetgrass
Powers: Protection, Healing, Psychism, Power, Lactation
Magical/Ritual Lore:

Long thought by ancients to be solidifed water or ice, quartz crystal has been used in religious and shamanistic systems for thousands of years. Because of its connection with water it has been utilized to magically create rain in many parts of the Pacific, including Australia and New Guinea.

Traditionally, quartz was utilized in the Eleusinian mysteries to produce the sacred fire by concentrating the heat of the sun to ignite wood chips. I say "traditionally" because we don't know much about these ancient, secret rituals.

Quartz was in common use among North American Indians in rite and spell, and ceremonial wands topped with quartz crystals have been found in southern California. Cherokee shamans, acknowledging the crystal's power, kept it wrapped in buckskin when not in use. At regular intervals it would be "fed" deer's blood. It is a common component of shaman's power bags or medicine bundles.

Contemporary Wiccans wear quartz, often combined with silver, during Full Moon rituals. Because it is also Goddess-symbolic, quartz crystal spheres are often placed on the altar during lunar rituals. Its icy cold temperature represents the sea.

Two quartz crystals can also be placed on Wiccan altars to represent the God and Goddess, the two primal, creative powers of the universe. Some place a natural crystal to represent the God and a sphere for the Goddess.

In shamanistic terms the quartz crystal is the shaman, and the shaman is the crystal. There is no difference between the two. As such it is the perfect tool of the shaman and is utilized in rituals throughout the world.

Mystically, quartz crystal is symbolic of the spirt and intellect of human beings.

Magical Uses:

Quartz crystals are currently enormously popular. Their use in healing, altering consciousness and magic have linked them to the spirit of the New Age. Long neglected by people in most of the world, save for their industrial applications, quartz crystals are today a huge commercial business.

Though general directions for cleansing stones were given in Chapter Seven of this book, there are a few herbs specifically used in conjunction with quartz in this capacity.

Sage (*Salvia officinalis*) and Sweetgrass (*Hierochloe odorata*), two North American healing and purificatory herbs, are both associated with quartz crystals and, in shamanism, are herbal counterparts to the stone. Make an infusion (tea) of either or both of these herbs by adding two tablespoons to nearly boiling water. Let it sit until cold, then add the newly acquired or negatively charged (i.e., a stone used in removing disease) crystals to the infusion. Let them sit for at least a day in the infusion, then dry and hold in your receptive hand. If the stone feels 'cleared', it is ready for magic. If not, return to the infusion until it has done its work.

Clear or "white" quartz crystal is perhaps best known to the general public for stimulating psychism. Though most crystal spheres sold today are plastic or glass, true quartz crystal spheres are also available, at fantastically expensive prices. Though well worth the cost to those who can afford them, crystals need not be worked by human hands to be magically effective, nor must they be *pure*, or free of inclusions.

In fact, many crystal scryers or gazers utilize the inclusions, veils and tiny prisms within crystals to entrance themselves. And simply gazing into any crystal point, i.e., a natural crystal, can produce psychism.

In the Renaissance most 'skrying stones', or crystal balls, were fashioned of beryl, not clear quartz crystal. However, crystal was used in magical operations. It was sometimes half-covered with pure gold and set on a base of ivory or ebony wood. This was used as an instrument of contemplation to awaken the psychic mind.

In 19th-century European magic, the crystal sphere was placed beneath the pillow to create a rapport with the scryer, enhancing its effectiveness.

A crystal sphere can be exposed to the light of the Full Moon to strengthen its powers. Before scrying, a tea of mugwort or chicory is sometimes drunk, and fresh mugwort rubbed on the crystal.

Attach a quartz crystal to a silver chain with its point downward, and you've fashioned a fine pendulum. This is a tool which links the arm holding it with the intuitive, or psychic, mind. Though there are many different systems of determining the pendulum's answers through its swing, here are two common ones:

Circling, either clockwise or counterclockwise: yes, or favorable conditions.

Side to side: no, or unfavorable.

or

Circling clockwise: yes, or favorable.

Circling counterclockwise: no, or unfavorable.

Side to side: no answer.

Ask the crystal how it will respond to questions and work with it. It is a powerful tool of the subconscious mind.

In the Yucatan a special class of diviners, consulted to ascertain the 'will of the Gods' and the spiritual nature of illness, utilize quartz crystal for divination.

The sphere is first cleansed by passing it through the fumes of smouldering copal (a gum resin collected in Mexico and Central America for magical and religious use). Additionally, or sometimes instead of this censing, the crystal is dipped into a bowl of rum to cleanse it and to awaken its powers. The diviner then studies the reflected flame of a candle within the crystal to determine the nature of the illness or problem.

A quartz crystal point carried or worn increases psychism. Placed beneath the pillow it offers psychic impulses in the form of dreams, which are the language of the deep conscious mind. It also ensures peaceful sleep.

Tumbled and polished quartz crystal stones are inscribed or

painted with runes and used as divination stones, and divinatory objects such as tarot cards are often stored with quartz.

Once known as "star stones" in early Britain, they were used in folk magic. Here's an old example: Gather nine quartz pebbles from a stream. Boil them in a quart of water from the same stream. Allow the liquid to cool naturally. Drink a small amount of this liquid each morning for nine days to help cure illnesses.

A similar technique involves placing a quartz crystal in a clear glass of fresh spring water. Let the glass sit in the Sun for a day, then drink the water to subtly improve your health.

Quartz crystal is also worn to relieve headache, and a small crystal is placed against the gum to give relief from toothache until dental treatment is obtained. It is also held in the hand to reduce fevers.

Throughout the British Isles crystal spheres of an inch in diameter were mounted in silver and worn as amulets against illness. In shamanic healing sessions, as well as home treatments, crystals are rubbed onto the afflicted part of the body to remove disease. When the session is over, the crystal is cleansed before reusing.

The crystal can be placed on a painful part of the body and left there to rebalance bodily conditions and to remove blockages of energies, which many say result in illness.

Though expensive, cups made of quartz crystal were considered the finest for drinking herbal medicines, and a small quartz crystal or tumbled stone can be safely added to any infusion or tincture to increase its effectiveness.

Throughout the world, crystal was considered a "milk" stone. It was either placed on babies or worn by their mothers to increase lactation and to ensure their babies' assimilation of this basic food.

For protective purposes this stone is worn, carried or placed in the home. In the 14th century the quartz crystal was engraved with the image of a man in armor holding a bow and arrow. The stone guarded its wearer and the place where it was situated.

Quartz crystal is used as a power amplifier during magic. It is worn or placed on the altar for this purpose. Wands of crystal or containing crystal are also quite popular at this time.

Thirteen crystals (representing the lunar year) or twenty-one crystals (thirteen Full Moons plus the eight ritual occasions of Wicca) can be used to physically construct the magic circle, in which Wiccan rituals and magical rites are held. Situate the crystals with the points facing inward for religious ritual, meditation or general magic, and with the points outward for defensive or protective magic. Quartz pebbles or tumbled and polished stones may also be used.

A 'crystal garden' can be easily fashioned if you have several crystals. Fill a large wooden or white earthenware bowl with white sand. Then set the crystals in the sand with their points upward. There are no other particular directions as to how to place the crystals, so use your imagination.

You may wish to trace a pentagram (five-pointed star) on the sand using a crystal, then place one at each point and one in the center. This confers magical protection.

Workers utilizing the power of the elements may use five stones, four aligned with the directions (which relate to the elements) with the fifth in the center, representing Akasha, or the fifth element. This will empower your elemental magic.

Crystals may be set up in spiral formation for use as a focal point during meditation. The spiral is symbolic of spiritual evolution and reincarnation.

The crystal garden is a place of power, an altar of stone magic, a meditative device, and a protective ward for the home.

In image magic performed in salt, earth, or damp sand at the beach (see *Earth Power*), runes or images can be traced with the tip of a quartz crystal. While drawing, send energy through the crystal to the image.

Of the colored forms of quartz, many (agate, amethyst, carnelian, chalcedony, citrine, jasper, onyx, sardonyx and others) are treated separately in this book, but those more commonly known as quartz are discussed here.

Blue Quartz (Energy: Receptive) is a fine peace and tranquility stone.

Green Quartz (Energy: Receptive) is utilized in prosperity workings to increase money or to provide an "easy life." It is also worn to stimulate creativity.

Herkimer Diamonds (Energy: Projective) are miniature, double-terminated quartz crystals. They are fine substitutes for diamonds in magic.

Rose Quartz (Energy: Receptive) is used to stimulate love and to 'open the heart chakra'. To attract love, wear a heart-shaped rose quartz. Its magical applications include promoting peace, happiness and fidelity in established relationships.

Rutilated Quartz (Energy: Projective) is an energy stone. Wear during magical rituals or place on the stone altar to increase the effectiveness of your magic.

Smoky Quartz (Energy: Receptive) is another mood elevator and is worn as a grounding stone. It overcomes depression and other negative emotions.

Tourmalated Quartz (Energy: Projective), quartz penetrated by black tourmaline crystals, is often worn to stimulate astral projection.

DIAMOND

Energy: Projective
Planet: Sun
Element: Fire
Associated Metals: Platinum, Silver, Steel
Powers: Spirituality, Sexual Dysfunction, Protection, Courage, Peace, Reconciliation, Healing, Strength
Magical/Ritual Lore:

Legend has it that Europeans first "discovered" African diamonds in a shaman's leather pouch. Though reports of this legend are sketchy, if it is based on fact the African shaman might have used his diamonds much as shamans in other parts of the world use quartz crystals.

Anciently, diamonds were worn as polished stones. They were treasured for their beauty, but it wasn't until recently that their dazzling appearance was created. After people discovered that applying a bit of pressure at the correct point on a diamond produced a facet, the stone was prized for its prismatic fire.

Today, the world's supply of diamonds is carefully controlled to maintain an artificially high price—a surplus of diamonds on the market considerably lowers their worth.

Such greedy measures haven't lessened the magical value of the diamond. Because these high prices keep many of us from experimenting with the ritual uses of diamonds, the magical substitutes listed in Part IV can be used with satisfactory results.
Magical Uses:

The diamond has a wide and varied magical repertoire. Worn, it promotes spirituality, even ecstasy, the shaman's ritual state of consciousness. It is often utilized in meditation and in spiritual pursuits.

When carried or worn the diamond promotes self-confidence in relations with the opposite sex. It is said to be potent for relieving or eliminating the root causes of sexual dysfunction. Worn for this purpose, it removes cultural (some might say patriarchal) blockages which have caused generations of women to be nonorgasmic. The diamond is a cleansing, purifying and releasing stone in matters of sexuality.

In India, women (presumably rich) wear an unblemished white diamond with a slightly black hue to ensure male children. It is also worn to conquer infertility.

Though the diamond is not a stone of love, it is worn to ensure fidelity and to reconcile quarreling lovers. Today it is, of course, the most popular wedding ring stone, due in part to aggressive advertising, but other stones are perhaps more appropriate. This usage has no ancient history.

Because of its hardness and associations with the Sun, the diamond is worn or utilized in spells to increase physical strength. In ancient Rome it was set in steel rings and worn with the stone touching the skin. This produced bravery, daring and victory. It is still worn today for courage.

In the ancient magic of India, a diamond set in a platinum or silver ring was worn for victory in battles and conflicts. It was also fastened to the left arm for this purpose.

The diamond, owing to its flashing nature, has long been regarded as a stone of protection. For the best results, and to ensure its wearer luck, the diamond should be faceted into a six-sided cut.

Rather surprisingly, owing to the above associations, the diamond is a stone of peace when worn. It relieves nightmares and encourages sleep at bedtime.

Try scrying with a faceted diamond in soft candlelight, dazzling yourself in its inner world of color and light.

EMERALD
Energy: Receptive
Planet: Venus
Element: Earth
Deities: Isis, Venus, Ceres, Vishnu
Associated Metals: Copper, Silver
Powers: Love, Money, Mental Powers, Psychism, Protection, Exorcism, Eyesight
Magical/Ritual Lore:
    The emerald, with its brilliant hue, is representative of our planet.

Because emeralds are one of the most expensive stones on the market, the magical substitutes mentioned in Part IV of this book can be used in their place.

However, inexpensive, low-quality emeralds are available, as mentioned in Chapter Six. Shop around. You might find just the emerald you need for magical purposes.

Magical Uses:

If you wish to bring a love into your life, buy an emerald and charge it with your magical need through your visualization, perhaps while placing it near a green candle. After this ritual, wear or carry the emerald somewhere near your heart. Do this in such a way that it cannot be seen by others. When you meet a future love, you'll know it wasn't the visible jewel that attracted him or her.

Emeralds are often utilized in business spells and rituals to promote sales and to increase the public's awareness of the firm.

The stone is worn to strengthen the memory (it was suggested for this use by the pseudo-Albertus Magnus in the 16th century) as well as to increase understanding and to produce eloquent speech.

The stone affects not only the conscious mind, but also the psychic (subconscious) as well, for it increases its wearer's awareness of psychic faculties. Because of this dual effect, the emerald is said to grant all knowledge of the past, present and future.

Throughout the world the emerald was worn or utilized in magic for protection. The stone was bound to the left arm with string to guard travelers. Emeralds were given to "possessed" persons to exorcise the evil entity within them. (Many of these persons were epileptic or asthmatic.)

Its soothing color caused emeralds to be used as gazing-stones to relieve bleary, tired or weak eyes, and to relax the optic nerve and restore normal sight.

Perhaps the most curious usage of emeralds comes from India, where ancient Hindu writings prescribe wearing the stone during sleep to halt nocturnal emissions.

For best results in magic, or so the old magicians recorded, an emerald should be set in silver or copper.

FLINT
Folk Names: Thunderstone, Elf-Shot, Fairy-Shot, Elf-Arrow, Adder-stone
Energy: Projective

Planet: Mars
Element: Fire
Associated Metal: Silver
Powers: Protection, Healing, Divination
Magical/Ritual Lore:

Flint, a term vaguely applied to varieties of opaque quartz, was widely used in religio/magical rites by American Indians. Among the Cherokee, for instance, flint was invoked by shamans prior to medicinal treatments.

One of the first trade articles of early peoples, flint was used extensively to make blades. Ancient flint knives, found throughout Europe, were and still are used as protective amulets. They were known as "Thunderstones" and "Elf-Shot," revealing that their origins long remained unknown.

The Irish set flint knives in silver and carried them to guard against mischievous 'fairies'. In Scandinavia flint knives were sometimes honored as family 'gods'. Beer and melted butter were poured over them, much as holy statues are revered in contemporary India.

Magical Uses:

As mentioned above, ancient flint implements are protective amulets. It is thought to be particularly potent when placed above the door.

If you obtain an ancient flint knife (or a modern replica), place it on the altar or hold during protective rituals.

Flint is used in modern-day Brazil in divining gold, water, gemstones and other underground treasures.

A modern American flint spell: To cure a headache, strike a flint several times. As the sparks fly, visualize the pain traveling out from your head, into the sparks and dissipating with them.

FLUORITE
Energy: Projective
Powers: Mental Powers
Magical Uses:

Fluorite is one of the New Age stones. It is becoming increasingly easier to obtain in stores.

Fluorite is found in various colors and in masses of interlocking, interpenetrating cubes. Single crystals that resemble two pyramids fused together at their bases are available for sale as well.

This stone has no long history of magical use; its influences are only now being discovered.

In general, however, fluorite seems to work with the conscious mind. It is useful for straightening your thoughts, for reducing emotional involvement in a situation in order to gain a more accurate perspective.

It strengthens its user's analytical abilities and is useful for theorizing and assimilating information.

Because it affects the conscious (intellectual) mind, fluorite quells strong emotions and smooths thought over the angry sea of desperation, depression or anger.

Some workers use fluorite to strengthen the effects of other stones.

FOSSILS

Folk Names: Sponge: Witch Stone; Ammonite: Snake Stone, *Draconites*
Energy: Receptive
Element: Akasha
Powers: Elemental Power, Past-Life Regression, Protection, Longevity
Magical/Ritual Lore:

Fossils are the remains—or the negative impressions—of ancient creatures and plants that perished millions of years ago. Through eons they have been transformed into stone. Because they were once alive, fossils are linked with Akasha, the fifth element.

In the mystic language of the psychic mind, fossils represent time, eternity and evolution. They are a tangible example of how nothing in nature—not even a prehistoric sea creation—is wasted. Energy cannot be destroyed, only manifestations of energy. Matter is transmutable.

The ritual use of fossils is ancient. Fossils have been found in Neolithic burial sites in Europe. Why were they placed there? We can only speculate. Protection? Guidance to the other world? Assurance of rebirth?

Fossils are used as power tools by shamans throughout the world to amplify energy. Many contemporary Wiccans place them on their altars because of their mystic significance.
Magical Uses:

On a hot, dusty morning, David Harrington and I were collecting fossils in a southern Californian desert. Ancient sand dollars, bivalve (clam) shells and clusters of intricate coral revealed themselves to us.

Stopping to rest at midday, we miraculously found a stream splashing over the reddish brown, crystal-filled rocks. While we were sitting by it, the resinous scent of a huge desert lavender tree drifted around us as we looked over our finds. We thanked the Earth for sharing its treasures with us. Fossils are bizarre, beautiful magical tools. Though not stones in the usual sense of the word, the minerals that replace the ancient creatures and plants create rocklike substances, and so fossils have a definite place in a work of stone and crystal magic.

In general, fossils are used as protective objects. They are placed in the home, or fashioned into jewelry and worn to increase your natural defenses. In Morocco, stones embedded with fossils are carried for protective purposes.

Due to their enormous age fossils of all types are also worn as amulets to increase the life span.

They can be placed on the altar as symbols of the Earth and the ambiguity of time, or to increase the power of magical rituals.

Some types of fossils have specific magical uses.

Ammonites, known in the Middle Ages as *Draconites*, are fossilized, spiral-shaped sea animals. Due to their bizarre appearance they were thought to be stones removed from dragon's heads, and were bound to the left arm for magical protection. In more recent times in Britain they were known as "snake stones."

Ancient sponges, sometimes found in Britain, are known as "Witch stones." They are round and pierced through with a natural hole. These fossils are strung and worn like beads or hung in the house for protection.

Fossilized sand dollars, which show a natural five-pointed design, are often found on Wiccan altars. They are linked with the pentagram, an ancient protective symbol, and the elements. Because they and all fossils are ruled by Akasha, the fifth element, these ancient sand dollars are carried or used in magic to gain awareness of the realms of Earth, Air, Fire and Water. Once this has been achieved, elemental magic can begin. (See Part IV for more information on the elements.)

A simple elemental spell: Before any rite, place a fossilized sand dollar in the center of your altar with one point facing away from you. Put a piece of turquoise near the right point and attune with the Earth.

Then, moving clockwise around the design, place a citrine, garnet and aquamarine at each point, representing Air, Fire and Water respectively. Attune with each element as you place the stones.

Finally, set a piece of jet, amber, or some other fossil or quartz crystal near the top point, representing Akasha. Call upon the elements collectively to empower your spell. Then perform the rite of magic.

If you don't have these particular stones on hand, use any of those listed under each element in the tables in Part IV.

Fossils are also utilized to recall past lives. Perform this ritual at night, and wear a quartz crystal to protect yourself from being unduly disturbed or magically harmed while in your psychic state. Meditate upon a fossil. Look at it, thinking of its incredible antiquity. Attune with it; feel its past-present time.

Next, in a room lit only by candlelight or with moonlight flooding in through the windows, hold a fossil in your receptive hand. Still your mind, breathe deeply, and awaken your psychic awareness.

Feel this life, this body, this personality slipping from you. Slide along the energy of your being ('soul') beyond birth, beyond death; beyond to another life.

If you relive a life or an experience disturbing to you, drop the fossil and you will return to the present.

I have mixed feelings regarding past-life regression, and I hesitated to include this ritual—simple as it is—in this book. This is an area fraught with self-delusion. Still, if you have an interest in these matters, it's far better to attempt a glimpse backward yourself, rather than trusting another to do it. Fossils can open the door.

Amber and jet, two other fossils, are discussed separately in this book due to their fame as magical tools.

GARNET
Energy: Projective
Planet: Mars
Element: Fire
Powers: Healing, Protection, Strength
Magical/Ritual Lore:
In the 13th century garnets were worn to repel insects.
Magical Uses:
The garnet, a fiery red stone, is worn to enhance bodily strength, endurance and vigor. It is worn or used in magic to tap extra energy for ritual purposes. Wear or carry one when exerting yourself (hiking

a mountain, studying until dawn, heavy ritual workings, and so on).

Because it is a projective stone, the garnet is worn for protective purposes. Five hundred years ago it was thought to drive off demons and night phantoms. Today the garnet, in common with many other protective stones, is seen to strengthen the aura and to create a shield of highly charged positive vibrations which repels negative energies upon contact. Say you're wearing a garnet at night and have visualized it protecting you. A would-be mugger, for example, might suddenly decide to let you pass by, "spooked" by the "bad vibes" you are releasing. Garnets are particularly prescribed as protection against thieves.

In the Middle Ages a figure of a lion was carved onto a garnet and carried to guard the health, especially while traveling.

A healing stone, garnet is used to relieve skin conditions, especially inflammations. It also regulates the heart and blood.

In the past garnets were exchanged between parting friends to symbolize their affection and to magically ensure that they met again.

GEODES
Folk Names: *Aetites, Echites, Aquileus,* Eagle Stone, Thunderegg
Energy: Receptive
Element: Water
Deity: The Great Mother
Powers: Meditation, Fertility, Childbirth
Magical/Ritual Lore:

In the Middle Ages geodes were thought to be favored by eagles, who placed them in their nests.

Round and containing crystals, geodes are egg symbols. They also relate to the Great Mother Goddess.
Magical Uses:

Geodes are hollow concretions containing crystals. All quartz crystals, for example, form within geodes, which may be a quarter-mile long or small enough to fit in your palm. Other geodes don't contain separate crystals but, when sliced, reveal intricate patterns of minerals.

Amethyst geodes are some of the most beautiful objects on Earth. When sliced or broken open, they reveal a mass of purple crystals growing in toward the center. Sunlight shining on them is dazzling. Elongated geodes, sometimes called "amethyst logs," are often available and are well worth the three- to four-figure price asked. They recall Merlin's cave as popularized in Mary Stewart's excellent Arthurian novel *The Crystal Cave*.

An amethyst geode, or any geode containing isolated crystals, can be held and used in meditation as a contemplative object.

Placed on the altar or held, geodes can be utilized to concentrate the powers of the specific type of stone contained within them. During magic, use your visualization to release these powers toward the magical goal.

They can be placed in the bedroom and charged with energy to increase fertility and to promote conception.

The pseudo-Albertus Magnus recommended carrying or wearing geodes to attract love and to avoid untimely birth (miscarriage).

HEMATITE
Folk Name: Volcano Spit
Energy: Projective
Planet: Saturn
Element: Fire
Powers: Healing, Grounding, Divination
Magical/Ritual Lore:

Hematite is a strange stone. It is heavy, solid, and silvery black. Its name alone is something of a mystery. To ancients, hematite was what we now know as bloodstone, so virtually all magical information relating to "hematite" in old books refers to bloodstone. This hematite, though, when worked on a lapidary wheel, "bleeds" and produces stains that look much like blood, or so I'm told.

Hematite is a fine, showy stone. In Italy and elsewhere, it is fashioned into necklaces which are sold as "volcano spit." Magical information relating to this stone is scarce.

Hematite possesses the curious property of "healing" itself. Make a small scratch on the surface of the stone, then rub your finger over it. The scratch may disappear.
Magical Uses:

Hematite is said to be powerful in drawing illness from the body. As with all stones, it is held in the hands while visualizing, then placed on the skin directly over the afflicted area. A necklace of small stones can also be worn for healing.

Hematite is worn for grounding and stabilizing purposes, and to focus the attention on the physical plane.

A scrying: In a darkened room, light a red candle. Settle before it and hold a large piece of hematite so that the candle's flame is reflected on it. Gaze at the reflection and visualize a question. The answer will come to you.

HOLEY STONES
Folk Names: Holed Stones, Holy Stones, Odin Stones
Energy: Receptive
Element: Water
Deities: Odin, The Great Mother
Powers: Protection, Anti-Nightmare, Health, Psychism, Eyesight
Magical/Ritual Lore:

In the Eddas, Odin transmuted himself into a worm and slipped through a hole in a rock to steal "the mead of poetry." Perhaps because of this myth, holed stones were known as "Odin Stones."
Magical Uses:

On a windswept day, I went on a long drive out of the city to a point of land jutting out into the Pacific Ocean. Crawling over jagged rocks flecked with seafoam, I reached the fairly isolated beach.

I stood on it, huffing, and looked down. There, showing plainly against the brilliant white sand were dozens of holey stones. I picked one up, thanked the Goddess for this gift, and took it home to place on my altar to represent She who is the Mother of all Creation.

Stones with naturally occurring holes produced by erosion, wind or wave action, sea creatures and by other means have long been prized as protective objects.

There are numerous folk uses for these stones. They were hung on the bedpost to prevent nightmares. In England, holey stones were tied with red ribbon and hung over the bed for the same purpose within recent years. This seems to be a true survival of ancient magic and may still occur today.

As a magical protectant, holey stones were worn around the neck, placed in the house or hung from the front door. Hanging one near where a pet sleeps guards it.

To assist the body's healing processes, charge a holey stone to absorb the disease. Place this stone in a tub of warm, salted water and soak in it for several minutes. Repeat once a day for a week. Cleanse the stone after this and repeat as necessary.

In England Wise Women employed holey stones in healing rituals for children. The Wise Woman rubbed the sick child's body with the stone, magically removing the disease because the stone absorbed it. This curious rite was also performed on adults to maintain their health.

Another power resident within holey stones is the enhancement of psychism. In a wild and lonely place, preferably by moonlight, hold a holey stone up to one eye. Close the other one and peer through the stone. You may see visions, ghosts, or nonphysical entities.

And finally, looking through holey stones—in broad daylight, even at home—is said to improve eyesight.

JADE
Folk Name: *Piedra de Hijada* (Spanish, "Stone of the Flank")
Energy: Receptive
Planet: Venus
Element: Water
Deities: Kwan Yin, Maat, Buddha
Powers: Love, Healing, Longevity, Wisdom, Protection, Gardening, Prosperity, Money
Magical/Ritual Lore:
Jade has been used to create musical instruments, including xylophones, gongs and wind chimes. When the stone is struck, it produces a resonant tone. Such instruments were used in ritual in China, throughout Africa and by the Hopi Indians.

Jade was and is a sacred stone in China. Altars of the Moon and Earth were fashioned of jade, as were images of Buddha and various deities. The stone was often included in grave goods in China because it was thought to lend vitality to the deceased. Jade carved in the image of two men was exchanged between males as a token of friendship.

In New Zealand, the Maori carve nephrite (a stone related to jade) into images of ancestral figures, usually set with mother-of-pearl eyes. Called *hei tiki*, these figures are worn on ceremonial occasions. The stone itself is considered to be fortunate.

Jade is believed to have power over the weather. It was thrown into water with great force in order to bring mist, rain or snow.
Magical Uses:
Jade is an ancient love-attracting stone. Carved into a butterfly, in China it is worn to draw love, or is given to another in the hope of obtaining love. It was a frequent engagement gift from woman to man. Jade is also presented by a man to his bride before their wedding.

The soothing green color of jade is also healing. Wearing the stone helps the body to heal itself while working through the underlying, nonphysical problems which manifested the disease. It is particularly helpful for kidney, heart and stomach complaints.

Jade can be used to prevent disease and health troubles. The ancient Mayans wore jade amulets to guard against kidney disease and bladder problems.

The Chinese sensed in jade the power to prolong life. It was carved into images such as bats, bears and storks and worn for this purpose. Likewise, jade bowls were used in meals because the Chinese believed the stone's energy permeated the food before it was consumed.

A piece of jade is worn while gardening to improve the health of the plants. Four pieces of jade buried along the garden's perimeter are also effective for this purpose.

Wearing jade can bring money into your life. Charge a jade pendant or ring with money-attracting energies, then wear it and consciously allow yourself to receive money. Create a positive attitude toward money and visualize yourself using it productively, creatively. Gloomy visions of the "problems" money brings will effectively cut you off from it.

When contemplating a business deal, hold a piece of jade in your receptive hand for a few moments. Be infused with its prosperous energies. Then decide which course to take.

Jade is worn, carried or placed against the third eye to receive wisdom. Wisdom, by the way, isn't knowledge. It is assimilated knowledge rightly applied or withheld. Jade strengthens the mental faculties and helps reasoning.

This stone is also protective, guarding against accidents and mishaps which proper attentiveness can avert. It is also placed on the altar with purple candles or worn during defensive magic.

Just for fun, here's an old spell: Take a perfectly square piece of jade. Carve the numbers 1, 8, 1, and 1 on the square, one number in each corner.

Mount the stone in pure gold. As the Sun rises, turn to face it and breathe on the amulet three times. Then say "Thoth" 500 times. Wait until sunset, then again exhale thrice upon the stone and repeat "Thoth" 500 times. Once this is done, the amulet is finished. Tie a red thread around it and carry with you to guard against others imposing their will on you.

JASPER
Folk Names: *Gug* (ancient Assyrian), Rainbringer (American Indian)

Energy: various (see below)
Planet: various (see below)
Element: various (see below)
Powers: Healing, Protection, Health, Beauty
Magical/Ritual Lore:

American Indians utilized jasper in rain-attracting ceremonies, hence its name "rainbringer." It was also used by the early inhabitants of the United States in divination.

A green jasper which had been engraved with the image of a dragon surrounded by rays was worn by an ancient Egyptian king, Nechepsus, to strengthen his digestive tract.

Magical Uses:

Jasper is a common stone, an opaque variety of chalcedony, which is a form of quartz. Found in a wide range of colors—red, brown and green being quite common—it has been used in magic since the earliest times.

Generally, jasper is worn or carried to promote mental processes and to restrain dangerous desires or whims which could lead to hazardous situations.

It is also a protective stone, against both physical and nonphysical hazards.

A piece of jasper held in the hand during childbirth guards the mother and her child. It is also worn to relieve pain, especially during childbirth.

Perfectly carved arrowheads of jasper are worn to attract luck to its wearer.

Each color has its own corresponding magical nature and uses.

Red Jasper: (Energy: Projective, Planet: Mars, Element: Fire) Red jasper was engraved with images of lions or archers and carried to guard against poison and to cure fevers. A fine protective stone, it is utilized in defensive magic, for it sends negativity back to the original sender. It is also carried or used during healing and health spells. Red jasper is worn by young women to promote beauty and grace.

Green Jasper: (Energy: Receptive, Planet: Venus, Element: Earth) This is a healing amulet and health talisman. Ring green candles with green jasper to promote the body's healing or to ward off ill-health. Wear to halt hallucinations and to promote restful sleep. It is also worn to become more sympathetic to others' emotional and mental states.

Brown Jasper: (Energy: Receptive, Planet: Saturn, Element: Earth) Wear brown jasper for centering and grounding, especially after heavy magical ritual, psychic or spiritual work. If you tend to live with your head in the clouds to the point of endangering your physical life, wear a brown jasper.

Mottled Jasper: (Energy: Projective, Planet: Mercury, Element: Air) Wear mottled jasper for protection against drowning. It is said to be especially potent for this purpose when carved with the image of an equal-armed cross, representing the powers of the four elements, of foundation and control.

JET
Folk Names: Witches' Amber, Black Amber
Energy: Receptive
Planet: Saturn
Elements: Earth, Akasha
Deity: Cybele
Associate Herbs: Lavender, Sage
Powers: Protection, Anti-Nightmare, Luck, Divination, Health
Magical/Ritual Lore:

Jet is fossilized wood millions of years old. It is a black, glasslike stone. Because it is black, it is associated with the element of Earth, but due to its organic origins, it is also related to Akasha.

Jet shares with amber the property of becoming electrically charged when rubbed. Due to its mysterious nature and electrical properties, jet has long been considered a magical stone.

When jet is continuously worn on the body, it is thought to absorb part of the wearer's 'soul'. While this is true of many stones, jet was presumed to be doubly powerful, and such stones were carefully guarded, for in the wrong hands they could be used to manipulate their original wearer.

Ancient Greek worshippers of Cybele, the goddess of growth and plants, wore jet to obtain her favors. Modern-day gardeners also wear jet to make their plants flourish.

Along with amber, to which it is magically 'married', jet was found in prehistoric gravesites. It was probably placed there to bring good fortune to the deceased or to guard the bones.

Contemporary Wiccan High Priestesses, especially those following the basic ritual patterns popularized by the late Gerald Gardner, often wear necklaces of alternating amber and jet beads.

Jet is a marvelous stone. But beware—much of what is sold as jet is actually black glass. Purchase it only from a reliable source.

Magical Uses:

Jet is receptive and therefore absorbs energies, especially negativity. This makes it a protective substance. It can be worn as beads, carried, or placed beside white candles during protective rituals. It is a fine household protectant when placed in the home.

Sea Witches and fishermen's wives in old Britain prized jet as a potent magical protectant. They burned it in the household fires as an incense to guard their absent husbands.

A small piece of jet is sometimes placed momentarily on a newborn baby's stomach to guard it. It is also a special traveler's amulet, worn to ward off dangers while on the road or in strange countries. During the Middle Ages jet was carved into images of beetles and worn for protection.

To guard against nightmares and to ensure a good night's rest, wear jet to bed, place a piece under the pillow, or hang it on the bedpost.

Jet also strengthens psychic awareness. Place small shavings of the substance in a clear glass bottle. Fill with water. Let this sit in the Sun for several hours until the water has warmed. Filter out the jet and drink this liquid just before trying to contact the psychic mind.

Tiny amounts of powdered jet are also added to psychic-type incenses. Or, pour powdered jet onto a glowing charcoal block, still your mind, and scry in its fumes.

An ancient divination utilizing jet is quite simple—if you have a large ax and a fireplace or barbecue pit. Place the ax head in the fire until it is red hot. Enchant or empower the jet. Have a question in your mind, or visualize a possible future endeavor that is troubling you.

When it has been heated, move the ax head away from the fire and cast the jet on it. If it burns, the answer is yes, or the course of action is favorable. If not, the ax and jet have determined that the reverse is true.

Jet is also utilized in health and healing spells. It is worn to maintain proper energy flow within the body to avoid ill-health. Jet is combined with blue candles during healing fires or is fumed with lavender and sage to promote health.

KUNZITE
Energy: Receptive
Planets: Venus, Pluto
Element: Earth

Powers: Relaxation, Peace, Grounding
Magical Uses:

At a recent gem and mineralogical show in San Diego, I stopped by a booth displaying dozens of beautiful pink and lilac specimens of kunzite. The stones ranged in size from an inch or so in length to huge pieces a half-foot long. The kunzites emitted a peaceful vibration which was apparent just standing near them.

"Hold this. Doesn't it calm you?" a woman asked her companion, pressing a small piece of the stone into his hand. He affirmed that it did. The price tag was a stressful $95.00.

Kunzite is a fairly "modern" stone—no ancient sources mention it. Yet it has quickly garnered acclaim and a few magical uses by those who have worked with it.

The best-quality kunzite seems to be the lilac-shaded pieces. From what I've been told, the color will fade if exposed to sunlight for too long. It is, as mentioned above, expensive—a quarter-sized piece I recently purchased cost $9.00.

Magically, kunzite is held or worn to induce relaxation. It releases tension, soothing those muscles in which we often carry the effects of daily stress. Passing the stone over tension-ridden parts of the body unknits the muscles.

If your work subjects you to pressure, place a piece on your desk or near your work station. Hold it in your receptive hand to de-stress. Kunzite kept in the car can help you relax during traffic snarls. If you feel rich enough, add a small piece of kunzite to car protection amulets to ensure that you don't cause problems while behind the wheel.

Like amethyst, kunzite is also a peace-inducer. Carry or gaze at it to calm anger, nerves or fear.

It is also a centering, grounding stone and so is worn or carried to 'come down to Earth'.

Kunzite may also be useful for attracting love. Many of its secrets still lay within it, waiting to be discovered.

LAPIS LAZULI
Energy: Receptive
Planet: Venus
Element: Water
Deities: Isis, Venus, Nuit
Associated Metal: Gold
Powers: Healing, Joy, Love, Fidelity, Psychism, Protection, Courage

Magical/Ritual Lore:

Lapis lazuli has timeless associations with kings and queens.

In ancient Sumer the stone was closely associated with the deities in general. Carrying it, its possessor bore the potent magical power of a deity, for the stone contained the force behind all divinity. Some said the stone contained the soul of the deity, who would "rejoice in its owner."

It was a popular substance for cylinder seals in Sumer. These were small round stones deeply carved with images of deities as well as their symbols. Cylinder seals were used as "signatures" by pressing the carved stone onto wet clay documents and were also prized as amulets and talismans.

Some believe that lapis lazuli, a beautiful royal blue stone with flecks of golden pyrite, combines the influences of Venus and Mars since pyrite is ruled by Mars. This isn't too convincing as the pyrite content is minimal and, in some pieces, is virtually nonexistent.

Magical Uses:

Lapis lazuli, a rather expensive stone, is healing and soothing. Simply touching the body with this stone improves your mental, physical, spiritual, psychic and emotional condition.

It is used specifically to alleviate fevers and diseases of the blood. Lapis lazuli strengthens the eyesight if habitually worn. Held in the hand during any healing ritual, or placed around blue or purple candles, the stone helps the magician focus energy toward the magical outcome.

If performing a healing ritual for a friend, hold the stone and visualize the sick person as a healed, healthy, whole human being. Visualize the energy streaming into the stone and, thus magnified and specified, onto the person.

Lapis lazuli is an uplifting, spiritual stone. Its deep blue color reflects its peaceful vibrations. It is useful for relieving depression and promoting spirituality, and it is a fine meditative stone. Lapis lazuli stimulates gentleness in its wearer.

This stone is used in rituals designed to attract spiritual love. Take an untumbled piece of lapis with a sharp edge. Empower the stone and a pink candle with your need for love. Then, using the lapis lazuli, carve a heart onto the candle. Place the stone near the candleholder and burn the candle while visualizing a love coming into your life.

Lapis lazuli is considered a potent fidelity charm and so is worn to strengthen the bonds that have grown between lovers.

Perhaps its most common use today is to strengthen psychic awareness. Lapis breaks the hold of the conscious mind on the sub-conscious (psychic) mind and allows intuitive impulses to become known. Wearing a necklace of lapis beads or holding a piece in your hand enhances your awareness of these often difficult-to-perceive impulses.

To generally increase your psychic awareness (i.e., your ability to tap into this information), wear lapis every day. Or use it only when scrying, gazing, consulting the stone tarot or otherwise utilizing symbols which speak to the psychic mind. Remember: such divinatory acts and the rituals associated with them are usually 'tricks' which are designed to relax the conscious mind.

Lapis lazuli is also a protective stone, especially for children. In contemporary India, lapis lazuli beads are strung on gold wire. The resulting necklace is worn by children to ensure health, growth and protection. It was once placed around children's necks to drive away frights and disturbing fantasies.

This courage-inducing influence is also utilized by adults and is perhaps due to lapis lazuli's psychic and protective properties.

Despite its somewhat high price, lapis lazuli is one stone every stone magician should own and utilize.

LAVA
Energy: Projective
Planet: Mars
Element: Fire
Deity: Pele
Powers: Protection
Magical/Ritual Lore:

The volcano is an ancient symbol of creation. Erupting, it represents the four elements at work: Earth and Fire mix to create lava, which possesses liquidity (Water). Smoke (Air) rises from the crater. When the lava contacts water, it creates new land as it cools, and extends the landmass into the sea. In many parts of the world, such impressive attributes have enshrined lava with magical properties.

Before the Europeans discovered Hawaii, lava rocks were used to build *heaiu*, which were centers of religious and magical activities. *Heaiu* (an *s* is not added to Hawaiian words to denote plurality) had different functions. Some were centers of healing, complete with herb gardens; others were devoted to fishing deities; and still others were the domain of the war god Kukailimoku, Kamehameha's famous patron deity.

Contemporary Hawaiians who still practice the old ways go to healing *heaiu* and search for bluish lava rocks. They wrap a *ki* (ti) leaf around the rock and place this on the earth, asking for a healing. This practice is still extremely common, and if you visit a *heaiu*, especially one devoted to healing such as Keaiwa Heaiu on the hills above Honolulu, you'll see leaf-wrapped lava rocks in abundance.

Every day, packages containing lava rocks picked up by uncaring tourists are mailed back to the Visitor's Center in the Hawaii Volcanoes National Park. They are often accompanied by letters detailing the hardships their takers have experienced since removing the rocks.

Pele, the ancient Hawaiian goddess of volcanoes, destruction and creation, is jealous of Her stones. Just taking Her stones without first giving Her an offering (such as *ohelo* berries; *ohia lehua* blossoms; taro, or *kalo*, root; or, in the modern world, bottles of gin) and then asking permission is still viewed as a sure invitation for metaphysical trouble.

Magical Uses:

There are two types of lava known around the world by Hawaiian names. *A'a*, a chunky, rough lava, is considered to be projective, or masculine. *Pahoe'hoe*, or smooth lava, is receptive, or feminine. The *a'a* is the most potent in magical protection, but both work well. Because of their volcanic origin, I've listed both types as having projective energies.

A small piece of lava placed on the altar or carried in the pocket is a potent protective amulet. For general household protection, ring a white candle with lava and burn for fifteen minutes each day.

For protection during suspected psychic attack, bathe in salt water. Then, using nine or thirteen small pieces of lava, sit on the ground or floor facing East. Beginning in the East, place each stone a few feet from you to form a circle completely enclosing your body.

Feel the lava's protective vibrations setting up sprays or fountains of glowing liquid lava that repels and sends consciously or unconsciously directed negativity back to its originator. Repeat as necessary.

LEPIDOLITE
Folk Names: The Peace Stone, Stone of Peace
Energy: Receptive

Planets: Jupiter, Neptune
Element: Water
Powers: Peace, Spirituality, Luck, Protection, Anti-Nightmare, Psychism, Love
Magical Uses:

Two- to three-foot masses of brilliant lilac stone lay shimmering in the Sun. Interpenetrating the rocks were clusters of pink tourmalines. The effect was stunning, awe-inspiring.

In the hills on the Pala Indian Reservation, about an hour's drive north of San Diego, lie pegmatite-rich areas. In these mountains are found pink, red, green and multicolored tourmaline, mica, beryl, morganite, hiddenite (green spodumene), kunzite—and tons of lepidolite.

Lepidolite is a purplish type of mica rich in lithium. It is a beautiful yet fragile mineral. Though it is found in forms hard enough to be carved into eggs and spheres, most of it easily crumbles. Some of it is shot through with pink tourmaline crystals.

Because it is not a gemstone, lepidolite has been difficult to obtain in stores. As more stone magic practitioners become aware of its properties, it will become increasingly easier to find.

This is a calming stone, suitable for relieving the stresses of everyday living. Rarely made into jewelry, it is usually carried for this purpose.

Lepidolite soothes anger, hatred or any other negative emotion. Simply hold the stone in your receptive hand for a few moments and breathe deeply. Or, to quiet the entire house, place lepidolite stones in a circle around a pink candle.

Due to its calming effects and its sometimes vividly purple color, lepidolite can be used in rituals or carried to promote spirituality.

This mineral is carried to attract good luck to its bearer. It also drives off negativity, though its protective properties aren't extremely strong.

To promote a restful sleep, free of nightmares, place some lepidolite near the headboard.

Some stone magicians are now using lepidolite to increase psychic awareness. An easy way to do this is to place a large piece of the mineral on your altar between yellow or blue candles. Settle down before this and work to break your conscious mind's dictatorship.

Pieces of pink tourmaline embedded in lepidolite are useful for promoting love or calming the negative emotions that often upset relationships. It is a stone of reconciliation.

MALACHITE

Folk Names: *Malaku* (Greek, "Mallow")
Energy: Receptive
Planet: Venus
Element: Earth
Associated Herb: Mallow
Powers: Power, Protection, Love, Peace, Business Success
Magical/Ritual Lore:

A piece of malachite is worn to detect impending danger. Legends say that this stone, in common with many others, breaks into pieces to warn its wearer of the forthcoming peril.

Magical Uses:

This beautiful green stone with bands of varying hues has long been used to lend extra energy during magical rites. Wear it, hold it, or place it on your altar to increase your ability to send power toward your magical goal. Anciently, it was thought to be most effective when engraved with a rayed Sun figure.

Though the stone is a tranquil green-blue, it is used in protective magic, particularly that involving children. Beads or pendants of malachite are worn to guard against negativity and physical dangers. Malachite is a traveler's guardian stone and is said to be particularly powerful in preventing falls.

Wearing a malachite necklace that touches your skin near your heart expands your ability to love and, so, draws a love to you. Or, utilize the stone in love-attracting spells. Set it on a piece of copper etched with the symbol of the planet Venus (♀), a circle with an equal-armed cross below it. Behind the stone, place a green candle and let this burn for fifteen minutes a day while you visualize yourself in a loving relationship.

Its deep green color is soothing. Gazing at malachite or holding it in your receptive hand relaxes the nervous system and calms stormy emotions. Malachite promotes tranquility and ensures sleep if worn to bed. Held, it dispels depression.

Small pieces of malachite placed in each corner of a business building or a small piece placed in the cash register draws customers. Worn during business meetings or trade shows, it increases your ability to obtain good deals and sales. It is the salesperson's stone.

MARBLE
Folk Name: *Nicomar*
Energy: Receptive
Planet: Moon
Element: Water
Powers: Protection, Success
Magical Uses:

Marble is a carbonate of lime. Coral, calcite, limestone, stalagmites, chalk, seashells and bones are all lime, though they have varying magical uses.

Specifically, marble is used in protective spells. An altar made of marble, in whole or part, is an ideal center of protective spells. (Some magicians use a slab of marble for the top of their altars.) Marble tables and fixtures are protective for the home. Marble can be carried or worn for personal protection, as it was in India.

Marble is also utilized in spells involving personal success in a general sense.

MICA
Energy: Projective
Planet: Mercury
Element: Air
Powers: Divination, Protection
Magical Uses:

Mica, a general term for minerals exhibiting paper-thin flexible sheets of crystals, is a common stone.

Take a piece of mica at least an inch or so square. While visualizing yourself possessing complete control over your psychic powers, hold the stone in full moonlight. Capture the glow of the illuminary on the mica's shining surface. Gently moving the stone in your hands, let its shimmer drowse your conscious mind. Expand your psychic awareness and determine future events.

Mica is also carried for general protection.

MOONSTONE
Energy: Receptive
Planet: Moon
Element: Water
Deities: Diana, Selene, Isis, all lunar goddesses
Associated Stone: Quartz Crystal

Associated Metal: Silver
Powers: Love, Divination, Psychism, Sleep, Gardening, Protection, Youth, Dieting
Magical/Ritual Lore:

The moonstone, a blue, white or pink opalescent feldspar, is intimately connected with the Moon in magical lore. So much so, in fact, that many use it in accordance with the lunar phases. Some say it is more magically potent during the waxing Moon and less so during the waning. However, others use this stone during the Moon's apparent lessening for divinatory rituals, such as the one described below.

Moonstone has long been dedicated to Moon goddesses. Wiccan ritual jewelry is often fashioned of silver and moonstones. A lunar wand can be constructed of silver tubing topped with a large moonstone. It is used for magical ritual.

Magical Uses:

This stone is receptive and love-drawing. Wear or carry a moonstone to bring a love into your life. On the night of the Full Moon and by its light, ring a pink candle with moonstone cabochons. Light the candle and visualize yourself in a loving relationship.

The moonstone is also prized for its ability to work out problems between lovers, especially those who have bitterly fought. Hold a moonstone, empower it with loving vibrations, and give it to your troubled mate. Best of all, share this ritual with him or her by exchanging stones.

Because of its associations with the Moon, the bringer of sleep, the stone is often placed beneath the pillow, or moonstone beads worn to bed in order to ensure restful sleep.

Like malachite and jade, the moonstone is associated with gardening. Wear during planting or watering or bury a small moonstone while visualizing your garden bursting with fertility. To entice a tree into abundant fruiting, tie or attach a moonstone to one of the tree's limbs.

The moonstone is also gently protective. Because the Moon seems to travel through the zodiac, its stone is a traveler's protective charm. Carry or wear when away from home, especially during travel over or on the water. This is a perfect gift for avocational or vocational sailors and friends leaving on cruises. Empower the stone with protective energies before presenting it. Moonstone rings can be worn while swimming for protection in the water.

Top Row: Jet, Obsidian, Smoky Quartz, Black Tourmaline, Hematite
Bottom Row: Red Jasper, Garnet, Rough Ruby, Bloodstone

Top Row: Tiger Eye, Amber, Red-Orange Agate
Bottom Row: Carnelian, Topaz, Golden Beryl, Citrine

Top Row: Aventurine, Malachite, Raw Emerald, Jade
Bottom Row: Green Tourmaline, Peridot, Watermelon Tourmaline

Top Row: Rose Quartz, Rhodochrosite, Turquoise, Aquamarine,
   Chrysocolla
Bottom Row: Lapis Lazuli, Sodalite, Two Fluorites, Amethyst

Top Row: Tree Agate, Moss Agate, White Chalcedony, Tourmaline
    Quartz
Bottom Row: Selenite, Raw Opal, Moonstone, Rutile Quartz

Left:
    Single Terminated Quartz

Right:
    Double Terminated Quartz

Azurite

Chrysocolla

Lepidolite

Geode

Olivine

Pink Calcite

Green Calcite

Sunstones

Holey Stones

Black Tourmaline

Pipestone

Fossils

Sugilite

Lava

Hematite

Cross Stones

Petrified Wood

Meteorite

Boji Stones

Staurolite

An old ritual to determine future events can be performed at least three days after the Full Moon. Hold a moonstone in your hands while visualizing a possible future course of action, such as selling a house or accepting a new job.

Then place the moonstone beneath your tongue and continue visualizing. After a few moments, remove the stone and end your conscious effort to retain the image. If it remains or if your thoughts continue to revolve around the possible act, it is a favorable one. If your mind turns to other matters it's better to take a different route.

If in doubt perform this rite once again.

Moonstone beads or pendants are worn during divinatory acts and produce psychism in general. Psychics keep moonstones with their tarot cards or rune stones to heighten their ability to use such tools. A quartz crystal sphere is also encircled with moonstones prior to scrying.

This stone is worn or used in rituals designed to renew or maintain a youthful appearance and attitude (which can be more convincing than outward looks).

If you're trying to lose weight, perhaps moonstones can help. Don't diet—reprogram your eating habits. Eat light meals at regular intervals, avoid sugar and fats, consume less red meat, load up on raw or steamed vegetables and fresh fruits—and wear a charged moonstone.

Three nights after the Full Moon, stand nude before a full-length mirror in bright light. Study your body closely, using another mirror if necessary. To successfully perform this magic, you must know yourself, accept your faults, and then allow yourself to change.

Be brutal with your visual self-analysis. See the areas you wish to reduce on your body. Visualize a new you—slimmer, in control of your food intake, fully alive.

Then, hold a moonstone in your projective hand while continuing to visualize the body and discipline you wish to have.

Rub the moonstone over the problem areas of your body, over the excess amounts of fat, visualizing them melting away. Draw it across your head to help control your urges to eat unhealthy and fattening foods.

Finally, wear or carry the stone with you at all times. When you feel the urge to eat cheesecake, take the stone in your receptive hand, breathe deeply for ten seconds, push the image of the food from your mind—and then grab a juicy peach or crunchy carrot stick.

MOTHER-OF-PEARL
Energy: Receptive
Planets: Moon, Neptune
Elements: Water, Akasha
Associated Metal: Silver
Powers: Protection, Wealth
Magical/Ritual Lore:

Mother-of-pearl is the lustrous, opalescent interior of various sea mollusks. Though not a stone, it has been included here because of its long use in magic. Mother-of-pearl has been used in ritual jewelry throughout the ages. Seashells were the medium of exchange (money) in many parts of the world where metals were scarce or lacking, such as Polynesia.

Since this substance is the product of a living creature—the exterior skeleton, or shell—it is related to the fifth element, Akasha. Collect mother-of-pearl (m.o.p.) yourself in stream beds or the ocean. Since commercial m.o.p. is obtained by killing the animal which created it, it is therefore rather risky to use in magic.

Mystically, it relates to the ocean, to depth and movement.
Magical Uses:

Mother-of-pearl is placed on newborn babies to protect them from the perils of their new existence.

It is also a fine substance to use in wealth, money and riches spells. Empower a bit of m.o.p. with your magical need for money. Anoint it with seawater (which contains gold) or a money-drawing oil, such as patchouly or cedar. Place a silver coin or any pieces of silver next to the shell. Wrap a dollar bill or green paper tightly around the m.o.p. and silver object and secure with green string.

Place this talisman on your altar between two green candles. Let them flame for ten to fifteen minutes while visualizing. Then carry the charm with you.

OBSIDIAN
Energy: Projective
Planet: Saturn
Element: Fire
Deity: *Tezcatlipoca* (Aztec, "Smoking Mirror" or "Shining Mirror")
Powers: Protection, Grounding, Divination, Peace
Magical/Ritual Lore:

Obsidian is simply lava that cooled so fast that the minerals contained within didn't have time to form. It is a naturally occurring glass.

The ancient Aztecs fashioned flat, square mirrors of this black glass for use in divination. According to legend the famous Dr. Dee, a magician-alchemist hired by England's Queen Elizabeth I, may have used one of these mirrors in his scrying sessions.

It was a popular material for fashioning stone knives, spear points and arrowheads, and when used for these purposes, it is often known as "flint." Such arrowheads have magical properties. (See FLINT.)

Magical Uses:

Obsidian is a grounding, centering stone. Hold it in your hands or place your bare feet on two small, polished pieces when you're flighty or can't seem to get your physical life in order. Remember— the physical is the path to the spiritual. Each is a reflection of the other.

Obsidian is effective when carried or used in protective rituals. One involves surrounding a white candle with four obsidian arrowheads that each point to one of the directions. This sets up aggressive energies which guard the place in which it is set up.

Spheres of obsidian, still fashioned in Mexico, are fine scrying tools. If you don't have good results scrying with quartz crystal, try a piece or sphere of obsidian. For some, the blackness of the stone allows easier access to the subconscious mind.

OLIVINE
Folk Names: Chrysolite, *Chrysolithus, Lumahai* (Hawaiian)
Energy: Receptive
Planet: Venus
Element: Earth
Associated Metals: Gold, Lodestone
Powers: Money, Protection, Love, Luck
Magical/Ritual Lore:

A savage storm bombarded the tiny, round island of Kauai. I braved the stinging wind and, moving past the ironwood trees, looked out on Lumahai Beach (where parts of the movie *South Pacific* were filmed). *Lumahai* in Hawaiian means "olivine." As huge waves crashed a few yards from me, I knelt on the sand and saw countless millions of small green crystals interspersed with fragments of coral, lava and shells. A year later I knelt at Ka Lae, on the Big Island of

Hawaii, and gathered larger olivine crystals from the red sand. Nearby were beaches composed solely of olivine.

I've talked to several rock experts and none agree with each other. The question? Olivine/Peridot. The two stones, some say, are identical; others say olivine has a more olivish tint and that peridot is greener.

The stones, no matter their source, seem to be nearly the same color; though to some, olivine is a bit darker green.

Since this question isn't yet settled to my satisfaction, I've included both stones in this book under separate articles.

Olivine is a green, translucent stone. It is volcanic in origin and is found throughout the world. As I mention in Part III, it was recently found in meteorites.

Magical Uses:

Olivine is a money-drawing stone. Ring green candles with the stone or wear to bring money into your life.

Olivine sand can be purchased in gift shops in Hawaii. If you happen to obtain some, add a pinch to money sachets or place some in your pocket while visualizing. Those involved in the business world can put a small amount of olivine in their desks or in the cash registers. Or, put your business card on a green plate and completely cover it with olivine sand. All these rituals can also be done with olivine stones.

Olivine has been used for protection since it is of volcanic origin. It deflects negativity directed toward its owner, and so it is often used as an amulet. Small faceted olivine stones set into gold rings are ideal protective charms.

The stone is also set in gold and worn for protection against thieves, as well as to create a positive outlook on life.

Olivine is also a love-attracting stone.

And finally, like all green stones, it is carried or used in spells designed to bring luck.

ONYX

Energy: Projective
Planets: Mars, Saturn
Element: Fire
Deity: Mars
Associated Stone: Diamond
Powers: Protection, Defensive Magic, Reducing Sexual Desires
Magical/Ritual Lore:

In times past, onyx was thought to be the manifestation of a demon imprisoned in the stone. This demon woke up at night and spread terror and nightmares to any persons within its range of influence.

This demon was also thought to provoke discord between lovers (though see below for the reason why "discord" might occur if this stone is misused).

Magical Uses:

Onyx is a protective stone worn when facing adversaries in battles or conflicts of all kinds—or while hurrying down a dark street at midnight. (Isn't it nice that magic is practical?)

In classical ceremonial magic, the image of the head of the god Mars or a figure of the hero Hercules was engraved on onyx and carried for courage.

Onyx is used for protection as well as defense against negativity consciously directed toward you. While such things as 'psychic attack' or 'hexing' are rare and often exist only in the mind of the 'victim', performing defensive rituals can be psychologically cleansing.

A defensive spell: Place a square mirror on your altar. Set a purple candle before it so that the flame is reflected in the mirror.

Empower nine onyx stones with reflective, or defensive, energy. Place one piece of onyx three inches from the candle's right side. Then place eight more stones in a semicircle around the candle, working from right to left, until the candle is half-ringed with onyx toward you, but is clear of it in front of the mirror.

Light the candle. Visualize the onyx as collecting the negativity and sending it into the candle's flame. Then see the flame acting as a lens, focusing the negativity and sending it into the mirror.

The mirror is a doorway onto the spiritual plane. The negative energy is sent through it back to the original sender.

Protection is conferred.

Onyx has been used to reduce the sexual impulses. This is dangerous, for sexual release is a natural part of life. When it is repressed, mental illness, physical illness, antisocial behavior, religious delusions and even murderous tendencies can result.

Natural sexual impulses exist for pleasure, for union with other humans and the divine, and for the continuance of human life. Suppression of them leads to hatred, isolation and a lessening of respect for all life forms.

However, in these times of risky sexual contact perhaps onyx can be used to help curb uncontrollable sexual urges. Sex, especially when regularly performed with new partners (one-night stands), can be psychologically addictive. This can lead to neglect of nonsexual matters, sexual dysfunction (impotency or frigidity), and disease.

If uncontrollable desire is a problem, lie down fully clothed. Hold a piece of onyx about two inches above your groin. Let its soothing, spiritual vibrations bombard you. Visualize yourself desiring less sex, remembering that quality—not quantity—is all that matters. Do this for a few minutes once a day—but for no longer than a week. Wait a week before repeating this ritual.

Then again, onyx can be used to quell sexual desire when there is no chance of quenching it with your sexual partner—for example, during long physical separations, illness or the last stages of pregnancy.

Though self-stimulation (masturbation) can and should be a natural, satisfying release, many of us need the energy exchange with another person for fulfilling sex. Societal training has also plagued us with the false notion that masturbation is dirty, unnatural, and the cause of disease.

If this is the case and you have no access to sexual relations, either awake your own sexuality or, failing that, empower a piece of onyx and hold it a few inches above your groin, visualizing your sexual desire lessening.

When your partner is again available to you, stimulate your sexual desire with a diamond or carnelian so as to fully enjoy the contact.

Both of the above techniques can be dangerous. They shouldn't be done without careful thought. Never continue using onyx to repress your sexual desire for longer than a month or two, and reopen the sex center afterward.

Don't let this scare you away from onyx, however. When empowered for protective purposes, for example, it affects the sex center in different ways. Sex is linked with the survival of our species. So, it "protects" life. Wearing onyx or utilizing it in protective rituals channels sexual energy into the stone and from there creates protection.

A safe but expensive alternative to the above rituals entails having a diamond—it doesn't matter how large or small it is—set in onyx. When the diamond (which is sexually arousing) is surrounded by the sexually inhibiting onyx, it symbolizes control over our sexual natures.

OPAL

Energies: Projective, Receptive
Planets: all planets
Elements: all elements
Deity: Cupid
Associated Herb: Bay
Powers: Astral Projection, Psychism, Beauty, Money, Luck, Power
Magical/Ritual Lore:

To many, the opal is a stone of misfortune, sorrow, and bad luck. This is a modern idea, however, and is untrue. A reference by Sir Walter Scott in his novel *Anne of Gierstein* to the misfortune associated with an opal is the cause of this unfounded idea.

Magical Uses:

The opal contains the colors as well as the qualities of every other stone. As such it can be 'programmed' or charged with virtually every type of energy and used in spells involving all magical needs.

In the past opals were used to create invisibility. The gem was wrapped in a fresh bay leaf and carried for this purpose.

Usually, stones (and herbs) linked with invisibility were actually used to promote astral projection, and the opal is ideal for this purpose. There isn't room in this book to describe the various techniques used to consciously separate the astral body from the physical, so consult a standard book such as Denning and Phillip's *Astral Projection*, published by Llewellyn Publications.

Opals are worn during astral projection for protection as well as to facilitate the process.

They are also used to recall past incarnations. Hold the opal in your hands and gaze at it. Move your attention from color to color within the opal until contact with the psychic mind is achieved.

Once this occurs, go into the past.

The stone is favored by many to develop psychic powers and is often worn in jewelry for this purpose. Earrings are ideal.

Opals are also worn to bring out inner beauty. A beauty spell: Place a round mirror on the altar or behind it so that you can see your face within it while kneeling. Place two green candles on either side of the mirror. Light the candles. Empower an opal with your need for beauty—while holding the stone, gaze into your reflection. With the scalpel of your visualization, mold and form your face (and your body) to the form you desire.

Then, carry or wear the opal and dedicate yourself to improving your appearance.

Fire opals are often used in drawing money. They can be carried or placed beside green candles which are burned during visualization. If you own a business, place a fire opal within the building after empowering it to be a magnet, to draw customers.

Black opals are prized by magicians and Wiccans as power stones. They are often worn in ritual jewelry designed to increase the amount of power aroused and released from the body during magic.

And finally, due to its flashing colors and beautiful, unique appearance, the opal is a luck-bringing stone.

PEARL
Folk Names: *Margan* (ancient Persian), *Neamhnuid* (Gaelic)
Energy: Receptive
Planet: Moon
Elements: Water, Akasha
Deities: Isis, Aphrodite, Freya, Venus, Lakshmi, Diana, Neptune, Poseidon: all oceanic deities, though pearl is more specifically goddess-oriented; also associated with sky goddesses
Associated Metal: Silver
Associated Stone: Ruby
Powers: Love, Money, Protection, Luck
Magical/Ritual Lore:

Pearl, like amber, jet, fossils, mother-of-pearl and other substances used in magic, is the product of a living creature. Since the oyster must be killed to remove the pearl, some believe there is a heavy debt incurred by those who engage in trafficking pearls and by those who wear and use them.

The choice is yours—to use pearls in magic if you can afford them, or not. In presenting this traditional magical information, gathered from around the world, I'm certainly not advocating their use.

Popular folklore naming pearls as bringers of bad luck might be connected with the violence of their collection. You'll know intuitively whether you can use them or not. I don't, and not only because I can't afford them.

The pearl's dramatic, unexpected appearance within an oyster has long inspired religious and magical lore; though in some parts of the world, pearls were considered nuisances to those eating oysters.

Mystically, pearls symbolize the Moon, Water, the center of creation, and the universe.

Once incredibly expensive, virtually all pearls are now "cultured" by the Japanese and are available at more reasonable prices. Naturally occurring pearls are no longer available, except those 100 or more years old. Unfortunately, cultured pearls, made by inserting a bit of rounded shell into a living oyster, are mostly shell, not pearl and aren't as magically potent as naturally produced pearls. But their magical uses live on.

Freshwater pearls, produced in Japan and the United States, have basically the same qualities as sea pearls.

Mythologically, pearls were dedicated by the Romans to Isis after her worship was imported there from Egypt. They were worn to obtain her favors.

They were thought to be the congealed tears of Freya in early Saxon religion, and the Goddess in ancient Syria was named the Lady of Pearls. Throughout the Mediterranean region, pearls were associated with various manifestations of the Goddess, the summation of all that is female, creative, and nurturing—the feminine aspect of deity.

Pearls were once believed to be raindrops swallowed by oysters. In early Chinese belief pearls fell from the sky when dragons fought among the clouds (i.e., during storms), and this relates to the raindrops notion. Dragons and pearls are closely associated in Chinese thought.

Magical Uses:

Pearls are intimately connected with the Moon, so much so that some will wear or use them in magic only at night, during the Moon's domain. Because of this connection with lunar energy they are usually worn by women and rarely by men.

They have long been used in love magic, either worn or carried to spread loving vibrations. In India, women wear pearls as a magical insurance for a happy marriage.

A simple money spell involves purchasing a cheap pearl, the cheapest you can find. After attuning with the pearl and giving thanks for the oyster's sacrifice, hold it tightly in your hand and visualize money flowing into your life. See yourself as using it wisely. Money is energy, and squandered energy leaves you little in return.

Still visualizing, throw the pearl into a stream, the ocean, or any moving water. As the pearl contacts the element, it begins the process of bringing your need into manifestation.

This ancient spell was once performed in a slightly different manner—the pearl was thrown into a pile of rubbish as an act of sympathetic magic. Obviously, anyone who can throw away pearls is rich. The action magically created the desired condition.

Throughout the South Pacific, pearls are used by swimmers and divers as a magical protectant against shark attacks. It is also a potent household guardian against fire.

For a general luck or good fortune attractant, set pearls around a ruby and wear.

At various times and in various parts of the world, pearls have also been used by their wearers to lengthen life, promote fertility, drive off demons, preserve health, instill courage and lend physical strength.

Pearls are found in different shades. Each color, of course, has specific magical uses: black pearls as well as those of blue tints are thought to bring luck to the owner (but not, naturally, the oyster). Pink pearls are worn to manifest an easy, comfortable life. Yellow pearls, to the Hindus, bring wealth, and red pearls promote intelligence.

PERIDOT
Folk Names: Chrysolite, Peridote, Peridoto
Energy: Receptive
Planet: Venus
Element: Earth
Associated Metal: Gold
Powers: Protection, Health, Wealth, Sleep
Magical Uses:

As mentioned in the "olivine" article, these two stones seem to be nearly identical. One authority told me that the only difference between peridot and olivine was that the latter came from Hawaii.

Be that as it may . . . .

To be most effective magically, the peridot was once set in gold. This makes a fine, if costly, protective amulet, which the ancients said guarded against enchantments, night terrors and illusions as well as the universally feared evil eye. This latter term is usually defined as being either envy or unconscious psychic attack.

Though long associated with the Sun, I've attributed it to Venus here because it seems more suited to this planet.

Peridot is worn or carried for general healing purposes. Several sources say that cups or other vessels made of peridot were used in healing because medicinal liquids drunk from them were more effective.

Peridot is said to promote healing of insect bites and to help in liver ailments.

The stone is used to attract love as well as to calm raging anger. It is also useful to soothe nervousness and to dispel all negative emotions. Because it is calming to the nervous system, it is also helpful in promoting sleep if worn to bed. Such usages date back to at least ancient Roman times, when rings of peridot were worn to relieve depression.

Its deep green hue suggests peridot's use in wealth-attracting spells. Additionally, all magical uses associated with olivine apply to peridot.

PETRIFIED WOOD
Energy: Receptive
Element: Akasha
Powers: Longevity, Past-Life Regression, Healing, Protection
Magical Uses:

Petrified wood consists of ancient trees that, eons ago, were covered with mineral-rich water. The water slowly dissolved the wood and replaced it with various minerals. This process produced what we know as "petrified wood."

It is a fossil and is ruled by Akasha.

Because of its great antiquity (fossilized wood is millions of years old), it is carried or utilized in spells designed to extend the life span or, alternately, to increase our enjoyment of, and evolution within, our lives.

Also, due to its age, petrified wood is used to recall past incarnations.

The "stone" is carried as a protective amulet because of its hardness and strange appearance. In earlier times it was thought to "scare off" evil. Today we view it as setting up barriers of energy which deflect negativity.

Petrified wood is also carried as a charm against drowning.

PIPESTONE
Folk Names: *Inyan-sha* (Sioux: *Inyan,* "rock"; *sha,* "red")
Energy: Projective
Planets: Mars, Sun
Element: Fire

Associated Herb: *Kinnickkinnick* (red willow bark)
Magical/Ritual Lore:

Pipestone, for centuries, has been used by the Sioux and Omaha in rite and magic.

This is a curious, circular stone, brick red with a natural hole piercing it. Because of its color it is sacred. (Red is the color of blood and, therefore, of life.)

To the Sioux, the pipestone is related to the North. Red is the color of that direction. Both are symbolic of the Earth and the blood of its children—people.

A Sioux legend: A huge flood innundated the prairies. A few people managed to escape by climbing a hill but the flood drowned them. The hill collapsed among the people, crushing them and forming a pool of blood.

The pipestone is the solidified remnants of that pool, and it is found in only one place in the world, in Minnesota. This substance not only symbolizes the Sioux people, it *is* them. Pipestone was and is still used to make sacred pipes, in which *kinnickkinnick* (red willow bark) is smoked during rituals.

Magical Uses:

If you are fortunate enough to obtain pipestone, regard it as a sacred object. It is only right to respect the ways of the Sioux and Omaha. A piece of pipestone can be placed in medicine or power bags or on the altar during rituals.

The stone can also be placed on the altar during peace rituals.

I would never dare to wear the sacred pipestone.

PUMICE
Energy: Projective
Planet: Mercury
Element: Air
Powers: Easing Childbirth, Banishment, Protection
Magical Uses:

Pumice, a volcanic product, is a curious substance. Light and rough to the touch (one soap boasts it contains pumice to help in cleaning dirty hands), it also possesses the unique property of floating on water.

At one time pumice was pressed into the hands of women during childbirth, or worn, to ease the passage of the new life into the outside world.

A banishing spell: Take a piece of pumice and hold it in your projective hand. Visualize the problem you wish to be rid of—a damaging habit, negative emotion, physical ailment, or unrequited love.

While holding the stone, through your visualization send the energy which is behind the problem into the pumice. You might imagine it as streams of thick, black smoke, the consistency of molasses, flowing into the light, porous stone.

Then throw the pumice into a lake, stream, the ocean or any body of water.

As it hits the water, it releases the problem and its root causes into that element. Floating on the surface, the pumice strengthens your ability to "rise above" any and all negative conditions.

If you do not have access to bodies of water, fill a large basin or bucket with water and perform the ritual; then pour the water, stone and all, onto bare earth.

Pumice can also be placed on the altar during protective magic or in the home as an amuletic sponge. Empower it with the property of absorbing negativity.

RHODOCROSITE
Energy: Projective
Planet: Mars
Element: Fire
Powers: Energy, Peace, Love
Magical Uses:

This beautiful pink stone is carried or worn to lend extra energy during times of extreme physical activity.

It is also soothing to the emotions and the body, de-stressing it. For a soothing bath, add a piece of rhodocrosite to the tub or wear the stone during the bath.

While this may seem to be opposed to the first magical usage listed here, remember that it is your empowering of the stone that fine-tunes it to your magical need.

Rhodocrosite is also carried to draw love.

RHODONITE
Energy: Projective
Planet: Mars
Element: Fire
Powers: Peace, Anti-Confusion

Magical Uses:

Wear rhodonite to be calm, to cast off confusion, doubt and incoherency.

Rhodonite is also a fine stone to wear or carry to shut down the psychic centers.

This reddish stone, usually veined with lines of black, can also be worn to promote balance within the stone magician, shaman or Wiccan.

RUBY

Folk Name: Carbuncle
Energy: Projective
Element: Fire
Deities: Buddha, Krishna (not to be confused with the modern expression of Krishna-centered reverence)
Powers: Wealth, Protection, Power, Joy, Anti-Nightmare
Magical/Ritual Lore:

The ruby fashioned into a cabochon of a specific shape was known as "carbuncle" centuries ago. There is no stone of this name, though many books list carbuncle as a separate stone. Another example of the strangely convoluted history of gemstones!

This beautiful stone was considered the most perfect offering to Buddha in China and Krishna in India.

A widely held belief: Dreaming of rubies indicates coming success in business or money matters. If dreamt of by a gardener or farmer, the ruby denotes a good harvest.

This stone is one of many that is thought to grow dark when danger or negativity approaches its owner or when illness threatens. Whether this was psychically viewed, symbolic, or an actual change in color or clarity of the stone is undetermined, but was probably a psychic phenomenon. In this sense the ruby can be used as a tool of scrying, as can most of the transparent stones.

Magical Uses:

Rubies are truly precious stones. Perfect specimens of a deep, blood red hue are outrageously expensive.

Lower grade, non-gem quality rubies are available at nominal cost and can be utilized in magic, as can the substitutions mentioned in Part IV.

In 13th-century magic, rubies were well established as wealth-increasing stones. They were especially effective if engraved with the image of a dragon or snake before using.

Ancient magic from India states that the possession of rubies helps their owner to accumulate other precious gems, perhaps because of the stone's wealth-inducing qualities.

Worn, the ruby was thought to convey invulnerability, or protection against all foes, wicked spirits, negativity, plague, fascination (magical manipulation), and famine. It was also a special mascot of soldiers, guarding against wounds in battle. Basically, the ruby strengthens the body's own psychic defense system when worn.

The ruby in the home guards it against storms and negativity, especially if first touched to the four outside corners of the house.

Similarly, touching trees or the boundaries of a garden magically protects them from lightning and the affects of violent storms.

Ruled by Mars, the ruby is worn during magical rituals to increase the energies available to the magician or placed on the altar beside a red candle to lend energy to you when you're feeling depleted or drained.

In a similar line of magical influence, wearing a ruby is said to increase the body's warmth.

Jewelry set with rubies is worn to banish sadness and negative thought patterns. Such jewelry also produces joy, strengthens will power and confidence as well as dispelling fear.

Placed beneath the pillow or worn to bed, it assures restful sleep, undisturbed by nightmares.

Star rubies, those rare stones with a naturally occurring six-pointed star, are thought to be particularly potent in protective and other forms of magic since a spirit was thought to dwell within it. Star rubies can also be used as divinatory tools by gazing at the crossed lines of light.

SALT
Energy: Receptive
Element: Earth
Deity: Aphrodite
Associated Herb: *Ki,* or *Ti, (Cordyline terminalis)*
Powers: Purification, Protection, Grounding, Money
Magical/Ritual Lore:

Salt has long been a sacred substance. Mined in the earth or evaporated from ocean water in shallow basins, it is intimately connected with life and death, creation and destruction, and the feminine aspect of Earth energies.

Salt is a mineral of crystalline structure and so has a place in this book. Look at salt through a microscope. It is composed of regular, six-sided cubes. This square structure relates salt to the Earth.

Its use in religion spans the ages. Salt was frequently offered to deities, being deemed acceptable because of its scarcity and purity. In some parts of the world, such as ancient Rome and Abyssinia, salt was used as currency.

Salt is necessary for life, and yet an overabundance of it causes death. Similarly, sowing salt in fields destroys their fertility. It is sterilizing, purifying and cleansing.

Related to the element of Earth (as well as to seawater, which is a combination of two elements), salt is a powerful magical tool. Salt water is sometimes used as a magical substitute for blood where called for in old rituals. (NOTE: any blood substitutes, such as apple cider or freshly laid, fertilized eggs, can be used in rituals of this nature. Opening veins is a needless, hazardous magical practice, and sacrificing any life forms is useless and plays hell with your karma. Besides, would you want to be sacrificed for another's magical ritual? The only exception to this is menstrual blood, which is utilized in contemporary female magic and mysteries as it was in the past.)

In contemporary Hawaii many still follow the old ritual of mixing *alae* salt (rock salt covered with iron-rich red earth) with water. This is sprinkled with a *ki*, or ti, leaf on persons, structures and building sites for purificatory purposes.

Those Mexicans still attuned with magic often hang in their homes and businesses a large wreath composed of garlic or aloe vera, to which small packets of salt are attached to spread protection and to draw money.

Magical Uses:

Salt is a fine grounding and cleansing material. To purify gemstones, place them in a bowl of salt and leave for a week or so (see Chapter Seven).

Add some salt to your bath water. This creates an alchemical change—you've converted a solid (the salt) into a liquid. Bathe in this mixture to create a similar change in you. Visualize your doubts, worries, illness (if any) and all negative energies which plague you as leaving your body and entering into the water, where they are neutralized.

If you prefer showers, place a small amount of rock salt and a half-handful of hyssop (*Hyssopus officinalis*) in a washcloth and scrub your body.

To protect a home, sprinkle empowered salt in the corners of each room, visualizing it sterilizing and burning away negativity.

Pour salt in a circle around you on the floor, visualizing the salt's energies spreading down into the earth and up above you to form a protective sphere of brilliant white light. Within this circle is a perfect environment to perform protective or defensive magic.

Tasting salt brings you firmly down to Earth. It closes off your psychic centers (if working to awaken your psychic mind, avoid salt in your diet). It is also a protective and purificatory act.

If you feel the need to focus your energies and attention, to take a "tunnel-vision" approach to life for a while, carry a bit of salt in a green bag. This is especially important for those who tend to concentrate solely on the spiritual and neglect physical necessities.

Rock salt is also added to money-attracting talismans and is used in such spells. A salt wealth spell: On your altar or a large plate, carefully pour salt to form a pentagram (five-pointed star).

Empower a green candle with money-attracting vibrations and place this, in a small holder, in the center of the pentagram.

Light the candle.

Next, empower money-attracting stones. Place one on each of the pentagram's points. Use stones such as:

> Tiger's-eye
> Peridot/Olivine
> Jade
> Lodestone
> Opal
> Pyrite

or any of the money-attracting stones listed in Part IV of this book.

Five of the same stones or any combination of these can be used. As you place each stone, starting at the top-most point of the pentagram, say something like:

I place this stone to draw money.

Let the candle flame for ten to thirteen minutes as you settle yourself before it, visualizing.

Repeat each day for a week. Then place the salt in a small green bag, add the stones and any drippings from the candle, and carry with you to continue attracting money. When you feel the spell has fully manifested, pour the salt into running water (a faucet will do if nothing else is available), bury the wax and cleanse the stones. It is done.

SAPPHIRE
Folk Name: Holy Stone, Star Sapphire: *Astrae*
Energy: Receptive
Planet: Moon
Element: Water
Deity: Apollo
Powers: Psychism, Love, Meditation, Peace, Defensive Magic, Healing, Power, Money
Magical Ritual/Lore:
The Greeks identified the sapphire with Apollo, and the stone was worn when consulting oracles such as the famous one at Delphi.
Magical Uses:
This stone is worn to stimulate the third eye for the purpose of expanding psychic awareness. The ancient Greek practice mentioned above seems to indicate that even they were aware of the sapphire's ability to tap the subconscious mind.

Sapphire is a guardian of love. That is, it promotes fidelity and attunes the feelings between lovers. Anciently it was also worn to banish envy, to promote positive social interaction and to reconcile with foes; sapphire can be used for all those purposes within any kind of relationship, not just marital.

Its onetime usage for promoting chastity is probably also related to this: chastity can be viewed as the lack of sexual activity outside an established relationship. Star sapphires are thought to be especially effective for drawing or inducing love.

Sapphire is a soothing deep blue hue. It is worn during meditation or contemplated upon to expand wisdom. When you wear it, the stone promotes peace. The author of the pseudo-Albertus Magnus manuscripts of the late 1300's stated that this stone, worn, cools the "inward heat," or anger.

Its use in defensive magic stretches back to antiquity. Once thought to "scare devils and evil" away, it is today worn in protective jewelry and during rituals designed to return negativity to its sender.

A related power attributed to sapphire is its legendary ability to guard its owner from captivity. Currently, it finds favor with those involved in litigation and legal matters, possibly because it banishes fraud. The stone will work only if its wearer is in the right.

The sapphire is utilized in healing the body, especially the eyes, which are strengthened by its presence. It also reduces fevers and, when pressed to the forehead, halts bleeding from the nose.

Sapphires are also worn as general health-protectants, for, as Budge says in *Amulets and Talismans*, the stronger and healthier a body, the less chance "evil spirits" (i.e., disease, infections) have to do harm.

An ancient work by Bartholmaeus says: "Also wytches love well this stone, for they wene (ween, "believe") that they may werke certen wondres by vertue of this stone." It is worn and utilized in rituals to strengthen the magician's ability to tap and send forth power.

Generally worn as jewelry, sapphires are also utilized in money and wealth-attracting rituals. In early ceremonial magic the image of an astrolabe was engraved on the gem to increase wealth.

Star sapphires are considered to be more potent, magically speaking, for all uses.

SARD
Energy: Projective
Planet: Mars
Element: Fire
Powers: Love, Protection, Courage, Facilitating Childbirth
Magical Uses:

Sard is a reddish yellow or brown variety of quartz (related to carnelian). It is thought to be more magically effective for women than for men.

In the 1300's, sard was engraved with the image of a grapevine (symbolizing male energy) and ivy (female energy). This was worn by women for good fortune and to draw love.

Ruled by Mars and of a reddish color, sard is also used in protective rituals and in defeating negative spells (hexes) as well as to promote courage. Courage, which is *knowing* that you can face any situation, is created by strengthening self-confidence and also the body's projection of personal power.

At one time sard was given to women in labor to facilitate trouble-free childbirth.

SARDONYX
Energy: Projective
Planet: Mars

Element: Fire
Deity: Mars
Associated Metals: Silver, Platinum, Gold
Powers: Protection, Courage, Marital Happiness, Eloquence, Peace, Luck
Magical Uses:

Sardonyx is chalcedony layered with brown sard. It is used in protective rituals and is worn to promote courage and fearlessness. In ancient Rome a figure of Hercules or Mars was engraved on the stone for this last purpose.

Sardonyx is used to promote good relations between lovers or married couples, ending domestic strife and promoting communication.

It is worn or carried for eloquence, especially by lawyers and those who speak to the public. Because of this, jewelry containing sardonyx can be worn to court to ensure that the wearer's testimony is clear and concise.

Worn or placed near the heart, it relieves depression and despondency, producing peace and joy.

Sardonyx was at one time engraved with an eagle's head, set in silver, platinum or gold, and worn to bring good luck.

SELENITE
Energy: Receptive
Planet: Moon
Element: Water
Powers: Reconciliation, Energy
Magical Uses:

Selenite is a clear, layered mineral, superficially resembling calcite.

Named for Selene, an ancient Moon goddess, it is exchanged between lovers for reconciliation.

The stone is also worn to lend energy to the body.

SERPENTINE
Folk Name: *Za-tu-mush-gir* (Assyrian)
Energy: Projective
Planet: Saturn
Element: Fire
Powers: Protection, Lactation

Magical Uses:

The above correspondences as to energy, planet and element are tentative as there is little information available about this stone.

Seals made of serpentine were carried in ancient Assyria so the gods and goddesses would send double blessings.

Serpentine is also worn around the neck by nursing women to regulate their milk supply.

Otherwise, its main use is guarding against poisonous creatures such as snakes, spiders, bees, scorpions, and other troublesome reptiles and insects.

This may seem rather useless, but think about it. Have you gone camping in the mountains or hiking through wooded areas in the spring? How about rock-collecting expeditions in the desert?

When we leave our artificial environments (our homes), we're subjected to nature in all its manifestations, including creatures that bite and sting us in defending their territory or lives. Don't get mad— bring along some serpentine and carry or wear it while tramping through the woods or exploring nature. Perhaps you can prevent such misfortunes.

SODALITE
Energy: Receptive
Planet: Venus
Element: Water
Powers: Healing, Peace, Meditation, Wisdom
Magical Uses:

Sodalite is a deep blue stone veined with white. It is often mistaken for lapis lazuli but lacks the golden flecks of iron pyrite often contained in the latter stone.

It is healing, especially for emotionally related diseases or those caused by stress, nervousness, anger or fear.

Wear or rub over the body to dispel fear and guilt. Wear or hold to still the mind, relax the body and calm inner turmoil.

It is a fine meditative stone and, when used conscientiously, promotes wisdom.

SPHENE
Folk Name: Titanite
Energy: Projective
Planet: Mercury

Element: Air
Powers: Mental Powers, Spirituality
Magical Uses:

This greenish yellow stone is rarely found in transparent crystals. It is seldom used in jewelry due to its softness. *Sphene* is a Greek word for "wedge" (describing the shape of its crystals).

When found, it is used to improve the mind and the processing of information. It is excellent for studying, theorizing and debating.

Sphene is also worn to promote spiritual enlightenment during meditation and mystic rituals.

SPINEL

Energy: Projective
Planet: Pluto
Element: Fire
Powers: Energy, Money
Magical Uses:

Spinel is found in black, blue, green and pink crystals and is rather rare.

It is used in magic to lend energy to the body; it's worn for that purpose. Spinel can be used to boost physical strength during periods of excess exertion.

The spinel is also used in spells designed to attract riches and wealth.

STALAGMITES, STALACTITES

Energy: Stalagmites: Projective, Stalactites: Receptive
Element: Earth
Magical/Ritual Lore:

Stalactites (which hang from cave roofs) and stalagmites (which project up from the floors of caverns) are produced by lime-rich water dripping into caves from above. Over eons, they produce masses of calcite familiar to anyone who has entered such a cave. Sometimes they meet and form columns of stone.

In the past they were thought to be petrified earth. One hundred years ago it was a common practice for cave visitors to break them off as souvenirs. Such needless, senseless destruction has, hopefully, ended.

Historically, small stalagmites and stalactites were carried, often in small bags, as amulets against negativity and "evil." Their phallic shape probably contributed to their protective properties, in the popular mind. This is ancient magic and is included in this book because of its historical interest. There's no reason to destroy the beauty of caves for magical purposes. Substitute any other protective stone.

STAUROLITE
Folk Names: Fairy Cross, Fairy Tears, Staurotide, Cross Stone
Elements: Earth, Air, Fire and Water
Powers: Protection, Health, Money, Elemental Powers
Magical/Ritual Lore:

Staurolite (from the Greek word *stauros*, "cross") has many legends surrounding it, most quite recent and related to Christianity.

These stones are twinned crystals which form into equal-armed crosses, or *x*-shapes. At least three presidents of the United States—Roosevelt, Wilson and Harding—carried staurolite as luck charms.

It is often stated that they are found only in the Blue Ridge Mountains of Virginia. In fact, they also occur in North Carolina, New Mexico, France and Scotland, and perhaps in many other localities.

In Brittany they were said to have fallen from the skies and were worn as charms.

Though the cross is usually associated with Christianity in the Western world, it was used in religion and magic centuries before this relatively "new" religion was formed.

Equal-armed crosses symbolize the interpenetration of the physical and spiritual planes, the combination of projective and receptive energies within our bodies and souls, and also sexual intercourse.

In magic, staurolite represents the four elements.

Magical Uses:

Staurolite specimens vary in appearance. When the twin crystals intersect each other at right angles, they produce perfect crosses with arms of equal length. These are the stones favored in magic. More frequently, however, they cross at varying angles.

Staurolite is worn or carried for protection against negativity, disease and accidents. One can be empowered and placed in the car for this purpose.

This stone is also worn to draw wealth and to energize the sexual drive.

To gain control over the elemental forces, wear a staurolite set in any electrum fashioned as a ring or pendant.

An elemental spell: Place a staurolite flat on the altar with one point upward.

Next, empower a small green candle with Earth energies: wealth, stability, foundation, and fertility. Enchant a yellow candle with Air energies: communication, movement, thought, freedom, wisdom, and spirituality. Then empower two more candles: a red one (Fire), visualizing will power, energy, sexuality, and strength; and a blue candle, charging it with Water energies such as love, pleasure, psychism, purification, fluidity, and healing.

Place all candles in small holders. Set the green candle near the top-most point of the staurolite, the yellow candle near the Eastern point, the Red to the South, and the blue to the West.

If desired, ring each candle with stones related to that particular element (see Part IV for elemental stones).

Now light the green candle, visualizing its powers. Do this with each candle in turn, Air, Fire, and Water. See yourself as having control over these energies. Vow to work on balancing the elemental forces within your being. Blend them within you.

Repeat once a day for a week.

SUGILITE (pronounced soo-ji-lite)
Energy: Receptive
Planet: Jupiter
Element: Water
Powers: Psychism, Spirituality, Healing, Wisdom
Magical Uses:

Sugilite is a relatively new stone. Its uses in magic are new as well, and much research and experimentation is being performed with this stone at the present time.

It is expensive and is a dense, purplish stone of a good, solid weight.

The stone seems to facilitate psychic awareness when worn or carried.

As with most purple stones, sugilite is also worn for healing. It is also contemplated or worn during meditation to increase awareness of the spiritual world and is also worn to obtain wisdom.

SULFUR
Folk Names: Sulphur, Sulfer
Energy: Projective

Planet: Sun
Element: Fire
Powers: Protection, Healing
Magical/Ritual Lore:

Sulfur is a yellow mineral. When burned it emits a powerful, familiar smell. This odor, and its coloring, has caused people to use it in magic for centuries.

During the height of ceremonial magic, sulfur was often burned to drive off "demons" and "devils." This was related to the concept that positive forces were attracted by sweet scents, while negative forces abhorred foul odors and would flee from them.

Later, sulfur was burned as a magical fumigant to protect animals and dwellings from "fascination," or magical enslavement.
Magical Uses:

Sulfur was prescribed until quite recently for colds, rheumatism and bodily pain. It was usually placed in a small red bag and worn around the neck.

Pieces of sulfur are also placed on the altar during protective rituals or in the home as a general magical 'ward'.

SUNSTONE
Energy: Projective
Planet: Sun
Element: Fire
Associated Stone: Moonstone
Associated Metal: Gold
Powers: Protection, Energy, Health, Sexual Energy
Magical/Ritual Lore:

There are at least two stones named sunstone. One is a form of translucent quartz which has a vaguely orange hue. This is the Oregon sunstone.

Anciently, a form of feldspar which was imported from India was known by this name. In a sense it resembles an orange opal, with a fiery, multicolored flash. This is the only one used in past times in magic.

In the Renaissance this stone was frequently associated with the Sun, due to its sparkling orange-gold colors. It was set in gold and worn to bring the influences of the Sun into the magician.

Symbolically, sunstone is linked with moonstone.
Magical Uses:

In researching this book, I came across several references to this stone but no concrete information. Finally, at a rock show I found a dealer who had some sunstones—the old feldspar-type sunstone. I said I hadn't seen them before, and he commented that he'd bought them 20 years ago. They were beautiful and I eagerly brought them back home.

Sunstone, like most sparkling, reflective stones, is protective. Place one in the home before a white candle to spread protective energies through the house.

A stone placed in a bag of healing herbs strengthens their energies. The sunstone is also carried or worn to lend extra physical energy to the body during times of stress or ill-health.

If worn near the sexual region, it stimulates sexual arousal and increases sexual energy.

Unfortunately, the sunstone's use in magic seems to have been largely forgotten. No modern stone magic book I've read refers to it, even in passing. If you find a sunstone, treasure it.

TIGER'S-EYE
Energy: Projective
Planet: Sun
Element: Fire
Associated Metal: Gold
Powers: Money, Protection, Courage, Energy, Luck, Divination
Magical/Ritual Lore:

Roman soldiers wore tiger's-eye engraved with symbols for protection during battle.

Magical Uses:

Tiger's-eye is a fine stone for promoting wealth and money. A simple money spell involves empowering several tiger's-eyes with your need for money. Use them to surround a green candle. Light the candle and visualize.

They are also carried for protection against all forms of danger. A tiger's-eye cabochon set in gold is a fine protective ring or pendant.

Ruled by the Sun and possessing a golden flash of light, tiger's-eye is worn to strengthen convictions and create courage and confidence.

This is a warm stone, and it promotes energy flow through the body when worn. It is also beneficial for the weak or sick.

Sit outside on a sunny day. Hold a tiger's-eye in your hands and gaze at the flashes of light. Still your conscious mind and look into the future. Or, use the stone as a tool to delve into past lives.

TOPAZ

Energy: Projective
Planet: Sun
Element: Fire
Deity: Ra
Associated Metal: Gold
Associated Stone: Tiger's-eye
Powers: Protection, Healing, Weight Loss, Money, Love
Magical/Ritual Lore:

The stones we now know as peridot and olivine were named topaz in the distant past.

It was used at one time to cause its wearer to become invisible.

Magical Uses:

Topaz is another of the gemstones used for protective purposes. It is considered a specific against envy, intrigue, disease, injury, sudden death, sorcery and negative magic, and lunacy. The stone was thought to be especially effective when set in gold and bound to the left arm.

Worn, it relieves depression, anger, fear, greed, frenzies, and all disturbing emotions.

Placed in the home, it is a charm against fire and accidents. When put under your pillow or worn to sleep, the topaz fends off nightmares and ends sleepwalking.

The topaz is used to relieve the pain of rheumatism and arthritis as well as to regulate the digestive system. Perhaps this is why the stone is also worn for weight loss.

Known as "lover of gold," the topaz is used to bring wealth and money. Combine with an equal amount of tiger's-eye. Empower and place these stones around a green candle. Burn the candle and visualize.

Wearing a topaz draws love.

TOURMALINE

Energy: various (see below)
Planet: various (see below)
Element: various (see below)
Powers: Love, Friendship, Money, Business, Health, Peace, Energy, Courage, Astral Projection

Magical Uses:

Tourmaline was unknown to ancient magicians and is today still little used in magic, though its popularity is increasing.

Tourmaline is a unique stone in many ways. It is transparent when viewed from the side of the crystal, opaque, from either end. When heated or rubbed to create friction, it polarizes; that is, one end will become positive and attract ashes or light straws, the other, negative.

The stone is found in a variety of colors, each with its own magical attributes. Some crystals possess two or three hues.

Pink Tourmaline: (Energy: Receptive, Planet: Venus, Element: Water) Pink tourmaline draws love and friendship. Wear to promote sympathy toward others.

Red Tourmaline (Rubellite): (Energy: Projective, Planet: Mars, Element: Fire) Rubellite, or red tourmaline, is worn to lend energy to the body. It is also used in protective rituals. Worn, it promotes courage and strengthens the will.

Green Tourmaline: (Energy: Receptive, Planet: Venus, Element: Earth) This stone is used to draw money and success in business. Place one in a piggy bank or coin purse. Green tourmaline is also worn to stimulate creativity.

Blue Tourmaline (Indicolite): (Energy: Receptive, Planet: Venus, Element: Water) Wear this stone to de-stress, for peace and restful sleep.

Black Tourmaline (Schorl): (Energy: Receptive, Planet: Saturn, Element: Earth) Usually too brittle for jewelry, black tourmaline is seldom commercially available. It is used for grounding purposes and to represent the Earth in spells relating to that element. It is also protective, for it absorbs negativity when charged for that purpose via visualization.

Watermelon Tourmaline: (Energies: Projective, Receptive; Planets: Mars, Venus; Elements: Fire, Water) Watermelon tourmaline consists of an interior of red or pink tourmaline encased in green tourmaline. A broken or sliced watermelon tourmaline looks much like the fruit for which it is named. This stone is worn to balance the projective and receptive (male and female) energies within the body. It is also a love-attracting stone and works best for this purpose when used by balanced persons.

Tourmalated Quartz: (Energy: Receptive, Planet: Pluto) Wear or place beneath the pillow to promote astral projection. Or, obtain a sphere of tourmalated quartz and, gazing at it, still your mind and project your astral body into the crystal.

TURQUOISE
Folk Names: *Fayruz* (Arabic, "Lucky Stone"), Turkey Stone, Turkish
   Stone, *Thyites* (ancient Greek), Venus Stone, Horseman's Talisman
Energy: Receptive
Planets: Venus, Neptune
Element: Earth
Deities: Hathor, Buddha, The Great Spirit (American Indian)
Associated Metal: Gold
Powers: Protection, Courage, Money, Love, Friendship, Healing, Luck
Magical/Ritual Lore:
   Turquoise is a sacred stone to many American Indian tribes. The Navajo used ground turquoise and coral in creating sand paintings to bring rain to the parched land. Other native inhabitants of the Southwestern United States and Mexico placed turquoise in tombs to guard the dead.

   The Pueblos laid turquoise under the floor in offering to the deities, when a house, or *kiva*, was built. A piece of turquoise was a nearly required tool in the Apache shaman's medicine, or power, bag. Other American peoples attached turquoise to bows to ensure accurate shots.

   Besides these and many more uses, turquoise has been prized for its beautiful color and potent magical properties.
Magical Uses:
   It is a protective stone. Turquoise carvings of horses and sheep are kept by the Navajo as potent guardians against negative magic.

   A turquoise ring is worn to guard against the evil eye, disease, serpents, poison, violence and accidents, and any and all dangers. Worn, it promotes courage.

   Horse riders wear turquoise to protect themselves from falls. For this purpose it is mounted in gold. They attach a second small piece onto the bridle or saddle to give protection to the horse.

   It is a valuable amulet for travelers, especially when venturing into politically volatile or dangerous places.

   An old ritual utilized turquoise to gain wealth. Perform this rite a few days after the New Moon when the crescent is first visible in the sky. Avoid looking at the Moon until the proper time.

   Hold a turquoise in your hand. Visualize your magical need—

money—manifesting in your life. Move outside and look at the Moon. Then directly shift your gaze to the turquoise. The magic has begun. Carry the stone with you until the money arrives.

Turquoise is also worn or used in money-attracting spells, such as placing circles or necklaces of turquoise around green candles and visualizing wealth. Given as a gift, it bestows wealth and happiness upon its receiver.

The stone is also utilized in love magic; turquoise is worn, carried or given to a loved one. It is frequently used to promote marital harmony, ensuring that the two persons involved blend with each other. Some sources say that if love fades in the stone's recipient, the stone's color will fade as well.

Wear turquoise to attract new friends, to be joyous and even-tempered and to increase beauty.

It is also a healing stone. It strengthens the eyes, alleviates fevers and reduces headaches. When turquoise is pressed against the diseased or troubled part of the body, the illness is visualized as entering the stone. Water into which turquoise has been dipped is drunk for its healing energies.

Turquoise rings and pendants are worn to promote and to protect the health; blue candles surrounded with turquoise are visualized as speeding the healing process. The stone is said to prevent migraines when worn.

Like all blue stones, the turquoise is lucky and is carried to attract good fortune.

ZIRCON
Energy: Projective
Planet: Sun
Element: Fire
Associated Metal: Gold
Powers: Protection, Beauty, Love, Peace, Sexual Energy, Healing, Anti-Theft
Magical Uses:

This is a somewhat confusing stone. It is found in many colors, but some of them have been artificially produced. It is known by various names. All have magical qualities.

Clear (or White) Zircon: A magical substitute for diamond, it is worn for protection. Use for clear thinking and to promote mental processes. A curious ritual: Kiss a white or clear zircon. If you are chaste (celibate), the stone will stay clear. If not, it will turn black.

Yellow Zircon (Jargon, Jargoon, Ligure): Wear to increase sexual energy or to attract love. Carry to drive away depression, to increase alertness, and for business success.

Orange Zircon (Jacinth, Hyacinth): Wear to increase beauty and to still fears and jealousy. Carried during travel, it guards against injury. Worn or placed in the home, it safeguards against theft; so keep an orange zircon with valuables. Set in gold, it is doubly powerful.

Red Zircon (Hyacinth): This stone increases riches if worn or used in such rituals. It also guards against injuries. A protective stone, it vitalizes the body, lends energy in times of physical stress, and heals. Worn, it draws pain from the body.

Brown Zircon (Malacon): Use for grounding and centering. Brown zircon is employed in wealth and money spells.

Green Zircon: Green zircons are used in money spells.

PART III

THE MAGIC OF METALS

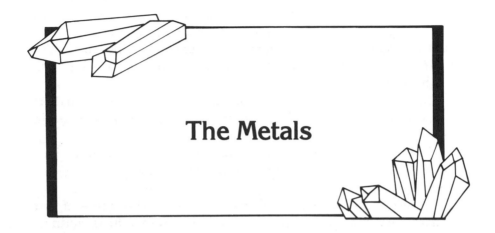

The Metals

A fireball flashes and roars across a primeval landscape. It strikes the ground with tremendous impact, sending up a cloud of dirt and debris. When it settles, the area is covered with smooth blackened objects of almost unreal weight. A human figure who has witnessed this phenomenon crouches warily, watching the sky, then stands and surveys the bits of strange material lying nearby.

The magnitude, the splendor and danger of the event triggers something in the witness' mind. After a long wait he or she guardedly snatches up one of the still-warm stones. Somehow, the witness feels, this is a powerful object, infused with the energies of the eerie points of light in the sky.

Ten thousand years later a priestess of the goddess Isis sits in a walled garden beside a lotus pool. She fingers a shiny metal image of a winged and kneeling figure. Silver, she muses, the metal of Isis.

Four thousand years hence a man strips off his clothing and carefully removes his glasses and brass bracelet. He changes into a robe possessing no metal zippers, no steel reinforcing tabs. He is preparing himself for magic.

Metals are 'the flesh of the gods and goddesses', the bones of the Earth, manifestations of universal powers. To our consciousness they may be expensive or common, beautiful or merely interesting, sacred or utilitarian.

All metals are potent magical tools. Their ritual use—or avoid-ance—is as old as magic itself. Just as early peoples sensed forces within stones, so too were metals found to contain energies which had tremendous influence. One guarded against evil. Another banished nightmares. A third was used solely in honor of the forces behind life and the universe.

Later, as humans devised the technology to free metals from their rocky matrixes, more sophisticated magical knowledge concerning metals evolved.

Today, metal magic is nearly forgotten, as herb and stone lore once was. This is unfortunate because metals are just as powerful and effective in magic.

Metals can be used alone or in combination with stones. If you are a lapidary or a jeweler, you can fashion your own magical rings, bracelets and crowns. If not, many potent pieces can now be obtained in stores, by mail or can be made to order.

The magic of metals doesn't require investing in a pound of gold or a ton of silver. Neither will you have to travel to distant lands in search of legendary mines. Metals are everywhere around us. To per-form this magic, all we need do is recognize the energies lying in wait within them.

PLANETARY METALS

Since at least ancient Babylonian times certain metals have been associated with the planets. This system, designed for ritual use, has remained fairly constant to this day.

To perform a spell related to one of the planets (see Part IV for planetary ritual information), empower its metal with your specific magical need and use it in some meaningful ritual way, just as you would stones.

Metals may be worn, carried, placed in small cloth bags, or situated near candles or stones—there are no limitations.

Keeping in mind that the ancients viewed the Sun and Moon as planets, here's a list of the heavenly bodies and their respective metals:

SUN—Gold
MOON—Silver
MERCURY—Mercury (Quicksilver), Electrum
VENUS—Copper

MARS—Iron
JUPITER—Tin
SATURN—Lead

Other metals have been discovered since those far-distant times (and planets as well), but this is the basic system. Full information on each of these metals is presented in the body of this section.

ELEMENTAL METALS

Though metals are obviously connected with the Earth, they are also attributed to each of the elements in order to provide another structure for ritual design. For magical influences of the elements, see Part IV.

EARTH rules Lead and Mercury
AIR rules Aluminum, Mercury, and Tin
FIRE rules Antimony, Brass, Boji Stones, Gold,
     Iron, Meteorite, Pyrite, and Steel
WATER rules Copper, Lodestone, Mercury, and
     Silver
AKASHA rules Boji Stones and Meteorite

Mercury, due to its peculiar properties, is jointly ruled by Earth, Air and Water. (See the article concerning this unique metal.) Electrum and other amalgams, or mixed forms, of metal are, obviously, governed by the elements which rule each of its components (i.e., an electrum of gold and silver is ruled by Fire and Water).

These two systems of ritual associations are, once again, tools which the magician can use in creating rituals. They are systems, not straightjackets!

On to discussion of the various metals.

ALUMINUM
Folk Name: Aluminium (British)
Energy: Projective
Planet: Mercury
Element: Air
Powers: Mental Abilities, Travel, Image Magic
Magical Uses:
     Aluminum is, perhaps, the most misused metal in modern times.

Aluminum cooking utensils have long been in vogue despite the apparent danger of the heat transferring certain elements of the aluminum to the cooked food, with possibly hazardous results.

Aluminum or forms of this light metal are found in everything from aspirin compounds to antiperspirants. It is used to create soft-drink containers and aircraft parts.

This is a "modern" metal with no history of usage among earlier peoples. Aluminum is sometimes recommended as an alternative to mercury, which is traditionally attributed to the planet of that name. It is certainly less dangerous to use, but don't cook in it.

In magic small pieces of aluminum can be carried to stimulate mental abilities. Due to its modern associations with travel, aluminum is also utilized in spells involving trips to distant lands.

Aluminum foil, which should be banished from every kitchen in the world, can be a tool of image magic.

Place a large sheet of foil on your stone altar. Light candles of the color which suits your magical need (see Chapter Four: The Rainbow of Power for specific magical information regarding colors as related to stones, candles and magical goals).

With your magical need in mind, form the foil into the proper shape. Let its shape fuel your visualization; send energy into and through it to bring your need into manifestation. When finished, smooth out the foil and douse with water. Dry, flatten and use the same foil every day. Repeat until you are successful.

Recycling aluminum is a new form of "magic," wherein we transform garbage into money. It's economically, ecologically and magically sound, so if you have a recycling center nearby, save your aluminum and transform it into "gold."

ANTIMONY
Energy: Projective
Planet: Sun
Element: Fire
Powers: Protection
Magical Uses:

Wear a small piece of antimony to guard against negative vibrations. This white metal can also be worn or carried for protection.

Bits added to combinations of protective stones strengthens their powers.

BOJI STONES*
Energy: Projective
Planet: Mars
Elements: Fire, Akasha
Powers: Power, Protection, Healing, Balancing Energies

On my recent trip to Denver, the owner of Isis Bookstore piled several bizarre-looking "stones" in my hands.

"Here," he said. "What are they?"

They were grey, metallic, heavy. Were they magnetic? No.

Some were grainy-surfaced ovals, fairly smooth, while others were studded with what appeared to be three-sided corners of some metal that had formed crystals within the "stone" itself.

A few were tubular-shaped, looking like two stones that had been smashed and fused together.

"What are they?" I asked, stumped.

"Boji stones," Leon said, smiling.

Yeah, I'd never heard of them either. They apparently come from some place in Kansas.

Holding one in each hand, I felt a tremendous flow of energy through my body.

Magical Uses:

Boji stones are something of an enigma. I've taken them to experts, but they aren't sure just what they are—crystalline forms of iron? Pseudomorphs (wherein organic or mineral substances are replaced with, in this case, metal)? At least one specimen, I was told, seems to be a fossilized vertebra of some ancient animal, in which the bone has been replaced with a form of pyrite.

Whatever they are, boji stones emit forceful, projective vibrations. They appear to be useful for balancing the body's energies, with the resultant effects of calming, grounding and healing. One women said that holding a stone in her hand had removed the pain from it.

They are certainly protective, in that they charge up our psychic defenses. As for their other uses, maybe we'll discover them together.

BRASS
Energy: Projective
Planet: Sun
Element: Fire

---

* Boji is a trademark of Boji Inc.

Associated Metal: Gold
Powers: Healing, Money, Protection
Magical Uses:

Brass has long been used as a magical substitute for gold. While it doesn't possess all of gold's attributes, brass is used in money-attracting rituals.

For example, at sunrise, empower eight small brass bells and eight green candles with your need for money. Do this in direct sunlight if possible. Place the candles (in holders) in a roughly square shape (two on each side). Ring each of the bells over each candle and visualize.

Or, place empowered olivine, aventurine or any other money-attracting stones on a piece of brass during prosperity rituals.

Another simple money-attracting spell: Inscribe a pentagram on a small piece of brass with a sharp nail or engraving tool, and carry or wear the brass piece to draw wealth.

Brass has also been used in ritual healing. Wearing a brass ring, for example, is said to halt stomach cramps. A brass key placed on the nape of the neck or dropped down the back is an old spell to stop nosebleeds.

This yellowish gold metal is also protective. Brass jewelry is worn to guard the person. It is used in defensive magic to send negativity back to its sender. Empowered brass objects are placed in the home for protective purposes.

COPPER

Energy: Receptive
Planet: Venus
Element: Water
Deities: Aphrodite, Astarte, Ishtar
Associated Stones: Quartz Crystal, Emerald
Associated Herb: Mimosa
Powers: Energy Direction, Healing, Luck, Love, Protection, Money
Magical/Ritual Lore:

Copper, a reddish orange metal, has long been linked with the divine. During ancient Mesopotamian times it was attributed to the Queen of Heaven as well as to goddesses associated with the planet Venus. These include Ishtar, Astarte and perhaps Inanna, the Sumerian predecessor to the first two deities mentioned above.

It has also been sacred to the Sun in Babylon as well as to the early inhabitants of the Pacific Northwest (U.S.).

Magical Uses:

Copper is well known as a conductor of electricity. One modern use of this metal is to fashion wands of copper tubes. These are topped with quartz crystals and sometimes wrapped with leather or another shielding substance. Such wands are used in magical ritual to direct energy. This metal is also worn during ritual for the same purpose—to heighten the magician's ability to direct energy to the magical goal.

Copper has long been used to stimulate healing. This seems to be because of copper's ability to balance the body's polarity, or the flow of the projective and receptive energies. Blockages in this energy pattern, according to shamans and healers alike, lead to imbalances and thus disease.

Copper's healing applications are boundless. In Mexico a copper penny is placed on the navel before a trip to prevent motion sickness. Copper is worn for relief of rheumatism, arthritis and any painful condition. Copper wire is loosely fastened around legs and arms to relieve cramps.

Pure copper in any form is often worn for general healing and to prevent sickness. To be most effective in health-related applications, copper is usually worn on the left side of the body by those who are right-handed, the reverse by left-handers.

Copper is a lucky metal, perhaps because of its past solar attributions, and so can be used in combination with any luck-bringing gemstones.

A metal of Venus, copper is worn to attract love. Emeralds, if you can afford them, can be set in copper and worn for this purpose.

Anciently, seeds of the mimosa (*Acacia dealbata*) were set into copper rings and worn, especially during confrontations, for protection against all manner of ills and negativity.

And finally, copper is used to draw money. Though the pennies of the United States are no longer made of copper, older pennies, especially those minted in leap years, have long been placed in the kitchen to attract money to the household.

ELECTRUM

Magical Uses:

Electrum is a general term describing a mixture, or alloy, of metals. Gold, silver and platinum are often found, in some combination or other, in electrum used in magic.

Naturally occurring electrum is rare and was once highly desired for use in magic. Today, even though electrum is produced through artificial means, this doesn't lessen its energies.

The process of mixing metals combines their powers. The "new" metal thus created is used in various magical operations, perhaps one requiring the combined forces of several different planets, or for a specific purpose.

Hundreds of years ago an electrum of gold and silver was fashioned into a cup. When a poisonous solution was poured into the cup, the electrum revealed its presence by emitting half-round rainbows and sparks.

While we needn't take this too seriously (though such an effect might be discerned through psychic vision), and certainly poisoning isn't as rampant today as it was in earlier times, this is an example of the powers attributed to electrum.

Ancient Egyptians made jewelry from naturally occurring electrum. Contemporary magical practitioners skilled in metalcraft make their own electrum for specific purposes.

For example, a Wiccan dedicated to the old Goddess and God of nature might wear a ring or pendant of silver and gold electrum. This would be symbolic of the unity of the two primal deities.

Today, electrum is rarely commercially available and usually must be custom-made.

GOLD
Energy: Projective
Planet: Sun
Element: Fire
Associated Stones: Quartz Crystal, Lapis Lazuli, Olivine, Peridot, Sardonyx, Sunstone, Topaz, Turquoise, Zircon (see articles on these stones for specific applications)
Associated Metals: Lodestone, Pyrite (see articles on these metals for specific applications)
Powers: Power, Healing, Protection, Wisdom, Money, Success, Male Sexual Dysfunction
Magical/Ritual Lore:

Gold is intimately linked with divinity, particularly with gods associated with the Sun. Throughout the ages, wherever it was found or obtained through trade, gold was often the material of choice for fashioning sacred images and decorating altars. It was also considered to be the highest offering to the deities.

During recent times gold has soared from an American value of about $30 an ounce to an incredible $1,000. Gold prices continue to fluctuate. Though the reasons behind this price increase need not concern us here, such worldwide interest in this precious metal is indicative of the power, if only financial, that gold possesses.

Today, gold continues to be the symbol of wealth and success to many. Gold jewelry is worn as if to say, "I'm successful." Few today seem to know its ancient magical properties.

When visiting cathedrals in central Mexico several years ago, I was amazed and saddened by the lavish use of gold on the altars. The meager wages of peasants have built monuments to the financial power of organized religion. In Mexico, as elsewhere, gold continues to be linked with religion.

Magicians working almost exclusively with solar energy wear gold ritual jewelry to attune with that power source. In Wicca, High Priests and those who revere the Sun as a symbol of the God often wear gold.

Legend states that the Druids collected mistletoe with sickles of gold. Herbalists in the Middle Ages also used gold implements during herb harvesting to strengthen the powers of the plants they collected.

Magical Uses:

Gold, perhaps the most magically potent of all metals, is utilized in magic to lend its energy to rituals. Worn during magic, gold jewelry enhances the magician's ability to rouse and send forth power. Wearing gold during your everyday life increases your personal power, thus promoting courage, confidence, and will power.

As mentioned above, gold tools were traditionally used to collect herbs. I say "traditionally" because pure gold is too soft for this purpose. If you happen to have some gold-plated knives lying around the house, they would be ideal for herb collecting. Strictly speaking, use these to gather projective (masculine, positive or electric) herbs. Silver knives are better suited symbolically for the collection of receptive (feminine, negative, magnetic) herbs.

Chains of gold are worn around the neck to preserve health, and gold bands are worn to alleviate arthritis. Gold worn habitually is said to ensure a long life.

Owing to its solar gleam, gold is a protective metal. Plain gold can be carried or worn as a guardian. A special ring made of gold and studded with gold nails is also protective. To this day small children in

India are guarded by tiny gold amulets. The gold crucifixes and crosses worn today by Christians are a survival of ancient Pagan customs.

During protective or defensive magic, place gold objects or jewelry on the altar. A simple gold chain placed around a white candle can be the focus of protective rituals.

Gold is also utilized to promote wisdom. For this purpose it is not carried but given to another, with no conditions. This is done to bring illumination to the giver.

Since it has long been used as a medium of exchange, and due to its great value, gold often figures in money rituals. This may seem strange. If you have gold, why perform money rituals? Actually, the smallest amount of gold, even a fragment of gold leaf, is all that is required. You might work out rituals involving gold, money-attracting gemstones and candles.

Gold-nugget jewelry is worn to bring a continuous flow of money into the magician's life, again by those fortunate enough to possess such rings. It is thought to be particularly potent for miners and for those investing in mines or precious metals.

As a symbol of the Sun gold is utilized in success rituals.

Wearing specially empowered gold has also been found to be helpful in relieving male sexual dysfunction (impotency).

IRON
Energy: Projective
Planet: Mars
Element: Fire
Deity: Selene
Associated Stones: Quartz Crystal, Holey Stones
Associated Metals: Lodestone, Meteorite
Powers: Protection, Defensive Magic, Strength, Healing, Grounding, Return of Stolen Goods
Magical/Ritual Lore:

Because iron is seldom found in pure form except in meteorites, the earliest iron available for use by humans was obtained from these strange celestial objects. Meteorites, which were observed falling from the heavens, were used to make simple tools, supplementing bone and stone implements by earlier humans.

Throughout most of the world, humans eventually learned how to remove iron from its ore, which made it available for wider use.

Once this occurred, it was soon limited to purely physical applications and was restricted in magic and religion. In ancient Greece, for example, no iron was brought into the temples. Roman priests could not be shaved or scraped with iron during bodily cleansing.

Ireland, Scotland, Finland, China, Korea, India, and other countries have severe taboos against iron. Again and again in ancient rituals fire was made without iron, altars built without its use, and magical rituals performed only after divesting the body of all traces of the metal.

Herbs were usually collected with non-iron knives, owing to the belief that the vibrations of this metal would "jam" or "confuse" the herb's energies.

The Hindus once believed that the use of iron in buildings would spread epidemics, and, even to this day, a gift of iron in any form is thought by some to be unlucky.

However, iron did have its place in magic. Specifically, it was worn or used in protective rituals. Its powerful, projective vibrations were thought to be feared by demons, ghosts, fairies, genii and other fantastic creatures.

In China, dragons were thought to fear iron. When rain was needed, pieces of the metal were thrown into "dragon pools" to upset the creatures and send them into the sky in the form of rain clouds.

In old Scotland, iron was used to avert danger when a death had occurred in the house. Iron nails or knitting needles were thrust into every item of food—cheese, grain, meat and so on—to act as a lightning rod, attracting the confusing vibrations that death may arouse within the living and thus sparing the food of possible contamination.

Classical Romans drove nails into their house walls to preserve their health, especially during times of plague.

Because of its protective effects iron was sometimes thought, conversely, to be sacred, and thieves in ancient Ireland wouldn't dare to steal it.

Magical Uses:

Iron—pure projective power, active, seeking, blinding, confusing, guarding.

For heavy protection, place small pieces of iron in each room of the house or bury at the four corners of your property. In earlier times, iron fences were sometimes used to halt the flow of negativity into the home.

During protective or defensive magic, wear an iron ring engraved with the symbol of Mars (♂). Or, obtain a three-inch thick white candle and eight old iron nails. Warm the nails by a fire (or in a red candle's flame), then thrust each into the white candle in a random pattern. Light the nail-studded candle and visualize yourself as guarded, protected, secure.

Wearing iron or carrying a small piece of this metal enhances physical strength and is an excellent talisman for athletes.

Iron is also used during healing rituals. A small piece is placed beneath the pillow at night. This was originally done to scare away the "demons" that had caused the disease but can be thought of as strengthening the body's ability to heal itself.

Iron rings or bracelets are worn to draw out illnesses from the body. This dates back to at least ancient Roman times.

A curious ritual from Germany to cure toothache: Pour oil onto a piece of heated iron. The fumes which rise from the iron will act on the problem.

In old Scotland, healing stones—quartz crystals or holey stones—were kept in iron boxes to guard against supernatural creatures who might steal them.

Iron is also worn for grounding, for closing down the psychic centers, and for impeding the flow of energy from the body. This, of course, isn't the best during magical ritual but is fine when the subject is under psychic or emotional attack, is physically depleted or wishes to focus on physical matters.

Iron horseshoes and the nails that attach them to the hooves are ancient magical tools. They might have first been used in ancient Greece, where they were called *seluna* and were associated with the Moon and the goddess Selene.

A horseshoe hung in the home over the front door confers protection. While theories differ as to the "proper" way to hang the horseshoe, I always place it points up. Ideally, it is to be nailed with three of its original nails.

An old iron horseshoe nail is sometimes bent into a ring (if you can find one long enough) and worn for luck and healing.

If you have had something stolen from you and have a fireplace handy, try this spell. Take a horseshoe nail that you've found by chance. Drive this into the fireplace, visualizing the stolen object returning to your home. It is done.

There are still magicians and Wiccans who remove all traces of iron from their bodies before working magic, but this custom is fading into oblivion.

LEAD
Energy: Receptive
Planet: Saturn
Element: Earth
Associated Herbs: Rose, Nettle, Rue, Cumin
Powers: Divination, Protection, Defensive Magic
Magical/Ritual Lore:

Lead has long been used in magic. In ancient Greek times tablets of this metal were ritually charged and inscribed with 'words of power'. These tablets were generally used in negative spells because the lead ensured the spell's long continuance.

In India during the 11th century, charms and figures designed to cause conception or to increase the fertility of gardens and orchards were engraved on lead tablets.

Magical Uses:

Lead is a heavy metal which causes death when it's absorbed by the body. The ancient Romans discovered this by using lead dishes and cooking utensils.

A curious divination, recorded in the 1800's in Italy by Charles Godfrey Leland, uses lead. Take three rose seeds (remove them from the "hip" that forms after a rose has lost its petals), three nettle leaves, two rue leaves and three cumin seeds. Put these on a metal plate along with a small quantity of lead.

At midnight, while clearing your mind of needless mental clutter, burn two yellow candles and light a fire. Place the metal plate over the fire. Then fill a large basin with water. Once the lead has melted, pour it, along with the herb ashes, into the water.

When the lead nodule has cooled, remove it from the water and gaze at its shape. The ritual and the lead itself should allow access to your psychic mind. If nothing comes to you, place the nodule beneath your pillow and let your dreams guide you.

Lead is worn or used in protective spells and also plays its part in defensive magic. It can be placed near the entrance of the house to prevent negativity from gaining access.

LODESTONE
Folk Names: Magnetite, Magnet, Way Stone, *Magnetis* (ancient Greek), Loadstone, *Shadanu Sabitu* (ancient Assyrian), Heraclean Stone,

Piedra Iman (contemporary Spanish)
Energy: Receptive
Planet: Venus
Element: Water
Associated Herbs: Sandalwood, Rose, Yarrow, Lavender
Associated Star: Polaris (the North Star)
Associated Stone: Coral
Associated Metals: Iron, Copper, Silver, Gold
Powers: Power, Healing, Attraction, Friendship, Love, Fidelity, Male
   Sexual Dysfunction, Will, Protection, Business, Money, Games of
   Chance.
Magical/Ritual Lore:

Legend has it that the ancient Romans had a statue of Venus made
of lodestone and an image of Mars fashioned of iron. When the two
statues were placed near one another in the temple, Venus attracted
Mars.

Tales (never substantiated) also sing the praises of a statue that
was permanently suspended in the air through the use of lodestones.

The stone was associated with the hero Hercules in times past
and so came to be a symbol of strength and invulnerability.

In contemporary folk magic, the lodestone is thought to be alive.
It is placed in a small bowl of water on a Friday to allow it to "drink,"
then laid in full sunlight to dry. When dry, iron filings are sprinkled on
it as "food."

Though there are variations on this procedure—some keep the
stone in a red bag and sprinkle water and iron filings on it once a
week—it is a common belief.

Several hundred years ago it was believed that it was dangerous
to carry a lodestone during a thunderstorm because it attracted
lightning.

A knife rubbed with the stone was not only magnetized, but any
wound inflicted with it, however small, was thought to be fatal.

The lodestone was once believed to be stripped of its magnetic as
well as magical powers by the mere presence of a diamond or garlic.
Giambattista della Porta, in his monumental 1558 work, *Natural Magic*,
said he had disproved such beliefs.

Nevertheless, some still believed this was true. Fortunately, there
was an easy way to restore the lodestone's powers. It was anointed
with linseed oil, placed in a goatskin bag and covered with dirt for
three days.

Its use to strengthen virility and to cure male sexual dysfunction (impotency) spans the ages. In ancient Assyria it was used in a sexual rite of pure sympathetic magic. The man placed a lodestone in oil and rubbed the resulting "infusion" on his body and penis to ensure satisfactory sexual intercourse. The woman rubbed *parzilli*, or iron powder, on her body to enhance her attractiveness. Thus prepared, couples three thousand years ago magically (or psychologically) released their inhibitions and shared pleasure.

Comparatively recently, in 16th-century India a king ordered his cooking utensils to be fashioned of lodestone to ensure his continuing virility.

Prostitutes once used lodestones to attract customers, and thieves relied on them to hide from authority.

All this lore has sprung from the lodestone's natural magnetic quality. It and artificially created magnets share the power of attracting iron. Five hundred years ago this was a magical, miraculous property, and many believed a spirit or demon lived within the lodestone and gave it power.

Though scientific investigation has explained magnetism to a certain extent, the lodestone continues to be used in spell and ritual. This is especially true in Mexico, where it is sold in *botanicas* along with candles, incenses, religious medals, snakeskins, oils and various other occult goods. Similar stores are found in many parts of the United States where Spanish-speaking peoples live.

Mexican street vendors who deal in magical supplies also sell lodestones. A few years ago I bought one from a woman who sat on the curb in a Tijuana district unfrequented by *turistas.*

It is also well known in Hoodoo and other American folk magic systems. Lodestones are sometimes painted green (for use in money spells), red (love), and white (protection). Painting them is not, of course, magically important unless you deem it to be so.

Magical Uses:

The lodestone is a power stone used to strengthen spells. It is added to sachets or herbal amulets, placed on the altar, or worn to increase the magician's ability to rouse and release energy.

In ceremonial magic of the Middle Ages the lodestone was engraved with the figure of an armored man. This stone was utilized during rituals to empower magic.

The larger the stone, the more inherent power within it. While this is true of all stones, it is especially important with the lodestone, for the greater its size, the stronger its magnetic force.

Lodestone's basic use in magic is *attraction*. Because the stone is a natural magnet, it is manipulated in ritual to draw objects or energies to its user. Thus, it can be used in any type of spell.

A simple example of this: A lodestone set in a man's belt buckle draws success in all undertakings. This is probably because of the stone's attracting qualities as well as its placement near what some call the 'third chakra', located about two inches below the navel. This energy center is associated with personal power and the will. When it is stimulated by the presence of the lodestone, it expands the will and therefore ensures success. This spell, by the way, is of Mexican origin.

The lodestone, owing to its magnetic powers, is used to draw out disease and pain from the body. True healers, who send energy into a sick person to speed the body's natural healing powers (or, specifically, to correct imbalances or blockages in bodily energy flows), may use the lodestone as a focusing device for their energies.

The stone can be passed over or placed directly on the afflicted part of the body. This is particularly true of pain in the hands and feet. It is also carried, often anointed first with a healing-type oil such as sandalwood. Any lodestones used in healing rituals to absorb disease should be cleansed after each use.

It is said to be effective in treating rheumatism and headaches, and in healing wounds. Placed in a black bag which was suspended on a black ribbon around the neck, it was a specific for gout a few centuries ago.

A small lodestone set in silver was thought to sharpen the sight. Set in gold, the lodestone strengthened the heart.

A folk spell designed to heal the body of any illness is quite simple: Hold the lodestone in your hands, then shake it vigorously while visualizing your illness draining from you and going into the stone. Bury the stone in the earth for a week following the ritual.

Any lodestone used in healing rituals to absorb disease should be cleansed after each use or, if worn, every week or so.

The lodestone is also worn or carried to attract friendship. If you've just moved to a new city or have started a job among unknown people, wear or carry a lodestone to meet new friends.

The lodestone is also utilized to attract love. It is thought to be a magnet for hearts as well as for iron, especially when worn in a ring. Place a pair of the stones within a circle of pink or red candles while visualizing yourself involved in a relationship. *Feel* the strong contact, the mingling of energies that comes with love. Visualize as well.

Two lodestones are also often carried in small red bags for this same purpose, sometimes mixed with love-attracting herbs such as rose, yarrow, and lavender (as well as copper, another love-inducer).

The lodestone is also worn to smooth over troubles in a relationship, especially arguing. Its basic function is to cool tempers to allow true communication.

A coral necklace with a lodestone suspended from it was once worn to facilitate easy childbirth.

In American folk magic, women wear lodestones to ensure that their wandering husbands will return home; thus, it stimulates fidelity. Since this borders on manipulation, as does all fidelity magic, it deserves a few words here.

When you begin a loving/sexual relationship with another person, and especially when children result, you have relinquished some control over your life to your mate and family. This is part of the giving involved in strong emotional ties.

At best such fidelity magic should be used to gently remind your partner of his or her obligations. If a relationship has ended, that's that—all the spells and lodestones in the world won't recapture the ecstasy, quiet peace and emotional fulfillment that love produces. Psychic or magical enslavement isn't love.

The lodestone's ability to overcome impotency has been mentioned above, but such drastic or complex methods needn't be used. A man suffering from sexual dysfunction can hold the stone in his receptive hand, visualizing satisfactory, complete, joyous sexual relations.

Once this is done, he can carry the stone with him or place it beneath the mattress to release its powers. The stone and the visualization work toward rooting out the underlying cause of the sexual dysfunction.

The lodestone has also been utilized as a protective amulet, being worn, placed in the home, or carried. A large lodestone surrounded by flaming white candles emits guarding energies throughout the house. It absorbs negativity but does not return it. Because of this such stones should be cleansed in salt water every Full Moon.

Some carry two lodestones at all times—one to protect, the other to bring good luck. In ancient Spain carrying a lodestone was thought to guard against all dangers from steel, lead, fire and water.

For those lacking in will power (which is simply asserting yourself and acting in accordance with your goals), empower a lodestone through your visualization with this specific directive: "Strengthen my will." Then carry the stone and utilize the energies it sends you. As I mentioned above, it can be worn two inches below the navel or placed there while you are prone and visualizing yourself as being confident and secure.

Because it is an attracting stone, the lodestone is used to draw money or business success. Place lodestone in a green bag with a silver coin, a bit of gold (if you have it) or money-attracting herbs such as patchouly, cloves or tonka. Business people may place an empowered lodestone in the cash register or cash box or burn green candles around a lodestone to bring in customers.

Finally, the lodestone is considered by some to be a potent gambling talisman. It is worn or carried for luck during betting.

MERCURY

Folk Name: Quicksilver
Energies: Projective, Receptive
Planet: Mercury
Elements: Water, Earth, Air
Magical/Ritual Lore:

Mercury—that strange, shining, molten "silver" that never solidifies. Mystically and magically mercury is a complex metal. It is possessed of a dual nature—projective *and* receptive, yang and yin, metal and liquid.

Due to its dense weight mercury is ruled by the element of Earth. Because it appears in a liquid state, it is also ruled by Water, and its rapid movements signify Air. Since Mercury is so poisonous this aspect could, perhaps, be ruled by Fire.

Let's face it, mercury is strange. It has been used in magic partly because of its unique appearance and properties.

For example, pools of mercury were once held in the hand and used as vehicles for scrying. Also used for this purpose were clear glass spheres, filled with mercury and tightly corked, then placed upside down on a stand.

A gambling talisman popular to this day consists of a hollowed nutmeg filled with mercury and sealed. This is carried for good luck with cards, dice, horses and numbers.

However—mercury is dangerous to breathe, ingest or even to

touch for prolonged periods of time. Its magical uses are therefore limited and, perhaps, needlessly risky.

The Witches' Almanac, a now-defunct annual publication that had great impact on Wiccans and folk magicians durings its years of publication from 1972 to 1980, printed a modern version of the Witches' bottle, an old protective charm, in the Aries 1976-Pisces 1977 edition. This charm consisted of three bottles. The smallest bottle was filled with mercury and placed inside another bottle. The second bottle was filled with water and then put into an even larger jar and covered with sand, rocks and shells.

After this spell was published it became immensely popular, and many started to use mercury in magic once again.

However, there are safer metals to use in magic—safer and cheaper as well. Don't use mercury. Please.

METEORITE
Folk Names: Aerolith, Aerolite
Energy: Projective
Planet: none, meteorites are associated with the Universe
Elements: Akasha, Fire
Deity: The Great Mother
Associated Stones: Peridot, Diamond
Powers: Protection, Astral Projection
Magical/Ritual Lore:

Meteorites have long been held in fascination by humans. They have been thought to be gifts from the gods and goddesses. Certain meteorites, such as the Kaaba stone in Mecca and a stone thought to represent the Great Mother Goddess of Phrygia, have been worshipped as symbols of divinity.

A four-ton stone has been revered in China as a holy object since the 1200's. The stone, shaped like a crouching ox, resides in a Bhuddist shrine. Recently, however, a team of Chinese geologists studied the stone and determined it to be a meteorite that landed about 1,300 years ago. The stone is no longer worshipped.

In Babylon the meteorite was a powerful magical protectant. It was thought to remove all evils due to its strange appearance and the "roar of its awful might."

Peridot is often found in meteorites. I held a small cut meteorite recently and studied the green peridot crystals that were packed inside it. The stone was worth about $3,000, so it didn't go home with me. Recently, tiny diamonds were found inside meteorites that fell in Mexico in 1969—the first discovered that had formed off of our planet.

At one place or another on Earth, meteorites were used to explain the origin of life. If rocks fell to the earth from space, so too could plants, water, animals and people.

Symbolically, meteorites can be viewed as the spiritual penetrating the physical, as astral power, divine order or whim, though a friend of mine says they're the melted remains of spaceships from distant galaxies!

Magical Uses:

Meteorites are unearthly things, literally. They possess the powers of intergalactic flight, of movement, of speed, and of energy unhindered by gravity.

Use them in rituals of protection. Place one on the altar near white candles; or carry in the hand.

They are also called upon to promote astral projection. A small meteorite or a fragment of one is placed beneath the pillow during attempts at conscious astral projection.

Yes, they are available for sale at reasonable prices. I visited the Reuben H. Fleet Space Theatre's gift shop in San Diego a few days ago and found small meteorites for $3.00.

PYRITE
Folk Names: Fool's Gold, Pyrites, Iron Pyrite
Energy: Projective
Planet: Mars
Element: Fire
Powers: Money, Divination, Luck
Magical/Ritual Lore:

Pyrite was used by ancient Mexicans in fashioning polished mirrors, which may have been used to divine the future. Pieces of this strange mineral were also placed in American Indian shamans' medicine bundles, perhaps to lend extra energy.

In ancient China this stone was used to guard against crocodile attacks, a problem which, fortunately, most of us seem to avoid without the stone.

Magical Uses:

Popularly known as fool's gold, pyrite is often found associated with real gold. So who, exactly, is the fool?

Because of the yellowish shimmer and shining nature of this "stone," it is used to draw wealth and money. Set five pieces of pyrite on your altar. Surround them with five green candles. Light the candles and visualize money coming your way, fulfilling your monetary needs.

Pyrite is also carried to bring money and luck.

A flat, shimmering surface of pyrite can be used as a magic mirror to awaken psychic impulses. Carried, it is a luck-bringer.

SILVER

Energy: Receptive
Planet: Moon
Element: Water
Deities: Isis, Diana, Luna, Selene, Lucina; all Moon and night goddesses
Associated Stones: Emerald, Pearl, Jade, Lapis Lazuli
Powers: Invocation, Love, Psychism, Dreams, Peace, Protection, Travel, Money
Magical/Ritual Lore:

Silver is the Moon's metal. Because it is found in its pure form, it was one of the first metals to be used by humans. The metal's beauty and scarcity caused it to be fashioned into divine images and offering pieces.

Throughout the world silver is identified with the lunar manifestations of the Great Mother, the eternal goddess. To this day Wiccan High Priestesses and those who view the Moon as a sacred symbol of the Goddess wear silver crescents in Her honor. Silver objects are also placed on the altar during Wiccan Full Moon rituals.

Worshippers of the Goddess may ring silver bells to invoke Her presence during rituals. Since the bell itself is a goddess symbol and since silver is dedicated to Her, this is a most effective and magically accurate ritual procedure.

Silver is also a popular protective amulet. In China small children are guarded by silver lockets worn around the neck. French couples about to be married are protected by a silver chain. The notion that silver bullets destroy vampires and werewolves has been spread by modern literature and the cinema.

Silver is the metal of emotions, of the psychic mind, and of love and healing.

Magical Uses:

Silver jewelry or empowered stones, such as emeralds, pearls, jade, or lapis lazuli, mounted in silver rings are worn to attract love. Or, etch the symbol of Venus (♀) on a small round silver disc. Place a pink candle over the disc and burn while visualizing love coming into your life.

Because silver is linked with the emotions, some feel over-wrought or emotionally overwhelmed if they wear it at the time of the Full Moon. If this occurs, be aware of it and, if necessary, wear some gold to balance yourself. Or, simply remove the silver.

Silver is also a psychic-influencing metal. When worn, it stimulates psychic awareness while lulling the conscious mind. Many psychics constantly wear silver in order to more easily tap into the subconscious.

On the night of the Full Moon scry with silver. Take any piece out into full moonlight. Compose yourself and hold the silver about two feet from your eyes, resting your hand. Catch the reflection of the Moon on the silver and gaze at this until psychic impulses become known.

Donning silver jewelry before sleep is one method of producing psychic dreams. If the piece is set with moonstones or any other psychic stone, its effects will be more powerful. An alternative is to place a piece of silver beneath your pillow. Still your mind as you lie above the metal. Visualize your need for a psychic dream. See yourself as remembering your important dreams in the morning.

If you are angry or nervous, wear some silver. There is an old belief that anyone touched with a silver ring, no matter what stone was set in it, would immediately become calm.

Silver is used for protective purposes. As the Moon reflects the light of the Sun, so too does its metal reflect negativity away from the wearer. Tiny silver globes (or any silver jewelry) are worn for magical security. Silver crescents, whose "horns" turn back evil, are popular worldwide.

This metal is also fashioned into jewelry, empowered, and then worn to keep its wearer's thoughts and moods in line.

Silver is said to be particularly potent in guarding travelers from dangers, especially while at sea.

Something like two-thirds of the world's population use silver (or silver-coated coins) as money. It is extensively utilized in money-drawing magic.

Empower a silver dime with money-attracting vibrations. If you don't have a silver dime, try a silver bead or some other small piece of silver. (Note: only those American dimes minted before 1965 are wholly silver.) Place this in or under a candleholder and then enchant a green candle. Burn the candle in the holder and visualize unexpected money flowing into your life.

STEEL
Energy: Projective
Planet: Mars
Element: Fire
Powers: Protection, Anti-Nightmare, Healing
Magical/Ritual Lore:
At one time steel was thought to offer protection against fairies, who could apparently be mischievous.
Magical Uses:
Steel is a relatively modern metal and has no great history in magic. However, some uses have been discovered and preserved.

For example, small pieces of steel are carried to guard against negativity. A steel ring is also worn as a protective amulet.

Hold any dull steel knife. Visualize it piercing and driving away negativity. Block negative impulses from disturbing you. See yourself waking up in the morning refreshed and rejuvenated.

Then place the knife beneath your bed and sleep over it. You should have no nightmares.

American folk magic: A steel ring worn faithfully on the hand prevents rheumatism. This, like many of these minor rituals, is rather difficult to prove!

TIN
Energy: Projective
Planet: Jupiter
Element: Air
Powers: Divination, Luck, Money
Magical/Ritual Lore:
An old Cornish spell states that to turn tin into silver, all the magician need do is place it in a tank of ants on a certain night of the Moon's cycle. Typically, the spell neglects to tell us which night—the first? The seventeenth? The twentieth?
Magical Uses:
Tin, metal of Jupiter, is used in a divination similar to that discussed in the article on lead.

On New Year's Eve, a prime night for foretelling future trends, melt a small quantity of tin in an iron cup over a flame (a gas jet will do).

Once the metal is melted, throw it into a bucket of icy water. Mop the floor, if necessary, then look at the metal's shape and at the folds or patterns that may be present on it.

Divine the future from the nodule.

Tin is also carried as a good-luck piece, and the metal may be shaped into money-attracting talismans such as minutely carved, tiny images of dollar bills.

PART IV

THE TABLES

The Tables

These tables summarize part (but not all) of the information presented in Part II. They are here for quick reference. Part IV is divided into six sections: Energy, Planetary Rulers, Elemental Rulers, Magical Intentions, Magical Substitutions, and Birthstones.

These tables correlate information on stones only, for time and space considerations. For metals, or further information on stones, check the Index.

Remember, these classifications are suggestions only. They work for me, but may not for you. Create your own system if this doesn't speak to you.

ENERGY

PROJECTIVE

Projective stones are energizing and are useful for healing, protection, exorcism, intellectual powers, luck, success, will power, courage and self-confidence.

Agate, Banded	Jasper, Mottled
Agate, Black	Jasper, Red
Agate, Brown	Lava
Agate, Red	Mica
Amber	Obsidian
Apache Tear	Onyx
Asbestos	Opal
Aventurine	Pipestone
Bloodstone	Pumice
Calcite, Orange	Rhodocrosite
Carnelian	Rhodonite
Cat's-eye	Ruby
Citrine	Sard
Cross Stone	Sardonyx
Crystal, Quartz	Serpentine
Crystal, Quartz, Herkimer	Sphene
Crystal, Quartz, Rutilated	Spinel
Crystal, Quartz, Tourmalated	Sunstone
Diamond	Tiger's-eye
Flint	Topaz
Fluorite	Tourmaline, Red
Garnet	Zircon
Hematite	

RECEPTIVE

These stones are soothing and de-stressing, and are related to love, wisdom, compassion, eloquence, sleep, dreams, friendship, growth, fertility, prosperity, spirituality, psychism and mysticism.

Agate, Blue Lace	Holey Stones
Agate, Green	Jade
Agate, Moss	Jasper, Brown
Alum	Jasper, Green
Amethyst	Jet
Aquamarine	Kunzite
Azurite	Lapis Lazuli
Beryl	Malachite
Calcite, Blue	Marble
Calcite, Green	Moonstone
Calcite, Pink	Mother-of-pearl
Celestite	Olivine
Chalcedony	Opal
Chrysocolla	Pearl
Chrysoprase	Peridot
Coal	Petrified Wood
Coral	Salt
Cross Stone	Sapphire
Crystal, Quartz	Selenite
Crystal, Quartz, Blue	Sodalite
Crystal, Quartz, Green	Sugilite
Crystal, Quartz, Rose	Tourmaline, Black
Crystal, Quartz, Smoky	Tourmaline, Blue
Emerald	Tourmaline, Green
Fossils	Tourmaline, Pink
Geodes	Turquoise

PLANETARY RULERS

SUN

These stones are useful in legal matters, healing, protection, success, illumination, magical energy and physical energy. Candles used in rituals with these stones are usually orange or gold.

Amber	Sulfur
Calcite, Orange	Sunstone
Carnelian	Tiger's-eye
Crystal, Quartz	Topaz
Diamond	Zircon
Pipestone	

MOON

These stones are suitable for use in rituals involving sleep, prophetic dreams, gardening, love, healing, the sea, the home, fertility, peace, compassion and spirituality. Candle colors: white or silver.

Aquamarine	Mother-of-pearl
Beryl	Pearl
Chalcedony	Sapphire
Crystal, Quartz	Selenite
Moonstone	

MERCURY

These stones are used for strengthening mental powers and for eloquence, divination, studying, self-improvement, communication, travel and wisdom. Candle color: yellow.

Agate	Mica
Aventurine	Pumice
Jasper, Mottled	

VENUS

Venusian stones are useful in rituals promoting love, fidelity, reconciliation, interchanges, beauty, youth, joy and happiness, pleasure, luck, friendship, compassion and meditation, and in rituals involving women. Candle color: green.

Azurite	Kunzite
Calcite, Blue	Lapis Lazuli
Calcite, Green	Malachite
Calcite, Pink	Olivine
Cat's-eye	Peridot
Chrysocolla	Sodalite
Chrysoprase	Tourmaline, Blue
Coral	Tourmaline, Green
Emerald	Tourmaline, Pink
Jade	Tourmaline, Watermelon
Jasper, Green	Turquoise

MARS

These stones are useful for promoting courage, aggression, healing after surgery, physical strength, politics, sexual energy, exorcism, protection, defensive magic and are suitable for rituals involving men. Candle color: red.

Asbestos	Rhodocrosite
Bloodstone	Rhodonite
Flint	Ruby
Garnet	Sard
Jasper, Red	Sardonyx
Lava	Tourmaline, Red
Onyx	Tourmaline, Watermelon
Pipestone	

JUPITER

These stones are fine for spirituality, meditation, psychism and religious ritual. Purple candles can be burned in conjunction with these stones in ritual.

Amethyst
Lepidolite
Sugilite

SATURN

Saturnian stones are useful for grounding, centering, protection, purification and luck. Candle colors: gray, brown.

Alum	Obsidian
Apache Tear	Onyx
Coal	Salt
Hematite	Serpentine
Jasper, Brown	Tourmaline, Black
Jet	

NOTE: In common with other authors and magicians, I've just started utilizing the energies of Uranus, Neptune and Pluto, the three planets unknown to the ancients, in magic. Magical information relating to them is limited at present, and opinions vary greatly. In the future more stones will be determined to be under the influence of these planets. In the meantime, here are lists of the stones I've tentatively placed under the rulerships of Neptune and Pluto. (Some of these stones are co-ruled by other planets.)

NEPTUNE

Amethyst	Mother-of-pearl
Celestite	Turquoise
Lepidolite	

PLUTO

Kunzite
Spinel
Quartz, Tourmalated

ELEMENTAL RULERS

EARTH

Stones related to this element are useful in promoting peace, grounding and centering of energies, fertility, money, business success, stability, gardening and agriculture. Candles used in conjunction with these stones should be green.

Agate, Green	Kunzite
Agate, Moss	Malachite
Alum	Olivine
Calcite, Green	Peridot
Cat's-eye	Salt
Chrysoprase	Stalagmite
Coal	Stalactite
Emerald	Tourmaline, Black
Jasper, Brown	Tourmaline, Green
Jasper, Green	Turquoise
Jet	

AIR

Air is the element of communication, travel, and the intellect. Its color is yellow.

Aventurine	Pumice
Jasper, Mottled	Sphene
Mica	

FIRE

Fire stones are used for protection, defensive magic, physical strength, magical energy, courage, will power (such as in dieting), and purification. Candle color: red.

Agate, Banded	Obsidian
Agate, Black	Onyx
Agate, Brown	Pipestone
Agate, Red	Rhodocrosite
Amber	Ruby

Fire, cont'd.

Apache Tear	Sard
Asbestos	Sardonyx
Bloodstone	Serpentine
Carnelian	Spinel
Citrine	Sulfur
Crystal, Quartz	Sunstone
Diamond	Tiger's-eye
Flint	Topaz
Garnet	Tourmaline, Red
Hematite	Tourmaline, Watermelon
Jasper, Red	Zircon
Lava	

WATER

Stones of this element are used in love rituals and for healing, compassion, reconciliation, friendship, purification, de-stressing, peace, sleep, dreams and psychism.

Agate, Blue Lace	Jade
Amethyst	Lapis Lazuli
Aquamarine	Lepidolite
Azurite	Moonstone
Beryl	Mother-of-pearl
Calcite, Blue	Pearl
Calcite, Pink	Sapphire
Celestite	Selenite
Chalcedony	Sodalite
Chrysocolla	Sugilite
Coral	Tourmaline, Blue
Crystal, Quartz	Tourmaline, Green
Geodes	Tourmaline, Pink
Holey Stones	

AKASHA

This is the 'fifth' element, and its stones are usually of organic origin, i.e., either substances from living creatures or fossils of long-deceased animals and plants. They are useful in a variety of magical applications, including longevity and past-life regression.

Akasha, cont'd.

Amber	Jet
Coral	Mother-of-pearl
Fossils	Petrified Wood

MAGICAL INTENTIONS

Included in this list are some of the stones recommended for use in rituals for various purposes. Not all magical intentions are listed here; for any others consult the Index.

ASTRAL PROJECTION
Crystal, Quartz, Tourmalated
Opal

BEAUTY
Amber
Cat's-eye
Jasper
Opal
Zircon, Orange

BUSINESS SUCCESS
Bloodstone
Malachite
Tourmaline, Green
Zircon, Yellow

CENTERING
Calcite
Zircon, Brown
(See also: GROUNDING)

CHILDBIRTH
Geodes
Pumice
Sard

COURAGE
Agate
Amethyst
Aquamarine
Bloodstone

Carnelian
Diamond
Lapis Lazuli
Sard
Sardonyx
Tiger's-eye
Tourmaline, Red
Turquoise

DEFENSIVE MAGIC
Lava
Onyx
Sapphire

DIETING
Moonstone
Topaz

DIVINATION
Azurite
Flint
Hematite
Jet
Mica
Moonstone
Obsidian
Tiger's-eye

DREAMS
Amethyst
Azurite

ELOQUENCE
Carnelian
Celestite
Sardonyx

FRIENDSHIP
Chrysoprase
Tourmaline, Pink
Turquoise

GAMBLING
Amazonite
Aventurine
Cat's-eye

GARDENING
Agate
Jade
Malachite
Zircon, Brown

GROUNDING
Hematite
Kunzite
Moonstone
Obsidian
Salt
Tourmaline, Black

HAPPINESS
Amethyst
Chrysoprase
Zircon, Yellow

HEALING/HEALTH
Agate
Amber
Amethyst
Aventurine
Azurite

Bloodstone
Calcite
Carnelian
Cat's-eye
Celestite
Chrysoprase
Coral
Crystal, Quartz
Diamond
Flint
Garnet
Hematite
Holey Stones
Jade
Jasper
Jet
Lapis Lazuli
Peridot
Petrified Wood
Sapphire
Sodalite
Staurolite
Sugilite
Sulfur
Sunstone
Topaz
Turquoise
Zircon, Red

LONGEVITY
Agate
Fossils
Jade
Petrified Wood

LOVE
Agate
Alexandrite
Amber
Amethyst

Love, cont'd.
Beryl
Calcite
Chrysocolla
Emerald
Jade
Lapis Lazuli
Lepidolite
Malachite
Moonstone
Olivine
Pearl
Rhodocrosite
Sapphire
Sard
Topaz
Tourmaline, Pink
Turquoise

LUCK
Alexandrite
Amber
Apache Tear
Aventurine
Chalcedony
Chrysoprase
Cross Stone
Jet
Lepidolite
Olivine
Opal
Pearl
Sardonyx
Tiger's-eye
Turquoise

MAGICAL POWER
Bloodstone
Crystal, Quartz
Malachite

Opal
Ruby

MEDITATION
Geodes
Sapphire
Sodalite

MENTAL POWERS
Aventurine
Emerald
Fluorite
Sphene
Zircon

**MONEY, WEALTH,
   PROSPERITY, RICHES**
Aventurine
Bloodstone
Calcite
Cat's-eye
Chrysoprase
Coal
Emerald
Jade
Mother-of-pearl
Olivine
Opal
Pearl
Peridot
Ruby
Salt
Sapphire
Spinel
Staurolite
Tiger's-eye
Topaz
Tourmaline, Green
Zircon, Brown, Green, Red

NIGHTMARES, to halt
Chalcedony
Citrine
Holey Stones
Jet
Lepidolite
Ruby

PEACE
Amethyst
Aquamarine
Aventurine
Calcite
Carnelian
Chalcedony
Chrysocolla
Coral
Diamond
Kunzite
Lepidolite
Malachite
Obsidian
Rhodocrosite
Rhodonite
Sapphire
Sardonyx
Sodalite
Tourmaline, Blue

PHYSICAL ENERGY
Beryl
Calcite
Rhodocrosite
Selenite
Spinel
Sunstone
Tiger's-eye
Tourmaline, Red
Zircon, Red

PHYSICAL STRENGTH
Agate
Amber
Beryl
Bloodstone
Diamond
Garnet

PROTECTION
Agate
Alum
Amber
Apache Tear
Asbestos
Calcite
Carnelian
Cat's-eye
Chalcedony
Chrysoprase
Citrine
Coral
Crystal Quartz
Diamond
Emerald
Flint
Fossils
Garnet
Holey Stones
Jade
Jasper
Jet
Lapis Lazuli
Lava
Lepidolite
Malachite
Marble
Mica
Moonstone
Mother-of-pearl
Obsidian

Protection, cont'd.
- Olivine
- Onyx
- Pearl
- Peridot
- Petrified Wood
- Pumice
- Ruby
- Salt
- Sard
- Sardonyx
- Serpentine
- Staurolite
- Sulfur
- Sunstone
- Tiger's-eye
- Topaz
- Tourmaline, Black
- Tourmaline, Red
- Turquoise
- Zircon, Clear
- Zircon, Red

PSYCHISM
- Amethyst
- Aquamarine
- Azurite
- Beryl
- Citrine
- Crystal, Quartz
- Emerald
- Holey Stones
- Lapis Lazuli

PURIFICATION
- Aquamarine
- Calcite
- Salt

RECONCILIATION
- Diamond
- Selenite

SEXUAL ENERGY
- Carnelian
- Sunstone
- Zircon, Yellow

SLEEP
- Moonstone
- Peridot
- Tourmaline, Blue

SPIRITUALITY
- Calcite
- Diamond
- Lepidolite
- Sphene
- Sugilite

SUCCESS
- Amazonite
- Chrysoprase
- Marble

TRAVEL
- Chalcedony
- Zircon, Orange

WISDOM
- Chrysocolla
- Coral
- Jade
- Sodalite
- Sugilite

MAGICAL SUBSTITUTIONS

This is a list of some magical substitutions for stones which you may not have on hand when you need them. Other substitutions are just as effective; these are some suggestions for the major stones.

Amazonite: Aventurine
Aquamarine: Beryl, Emerald
Aventurine: Amazonite
Beryl: Aquamarine, Emerald
Carnelian: Coral, Red Jasper, Sard
Cat's-eye: Tiger's-eye
Chrysocolla: Turquoise
Citrine: Topaz
Coral: Carnelian, Red Jasper
Cross Stone: Staurolite
Diamond: Herkimer Diamond, Quartz Crystal, Zircon
Emerald: Aquamarine, Beryl, Green Tourmaline, Peridot
Garnet: Red Tourmaline, Ruby
Jade: Green Jasper, Green Tourmaline
Jasper, Green: Jade
Jasper, Red: Carnelian
Jet: Obsidian
Kunzite: Pink Tourmaline
Lapis Lazuli: Sodalite
Moonstone: Mother-of-pearl
Olivine: Green Tourmaline, Peridot
Pearl: Moonstone, Mother-of-pearl
Peridot: Green Tourmaline, Olivine
Ruby: Garnet, Red Tourmaline
Sapphire: Amethyst, Blue Tourmaline, Blue Zircon
Sard: Carnelian
Sodalite: Lapis Lazuli
Staurolite: Cross Stone
Sugilite: Lapis Lazuli
Sunstone: Carnelian
Tiger's-eye: Cat's-eye
Topaz: Citrine, Yellow Tourmaline

Tourmaline, Blue: Blue Zircon
Tourmaline, Green: Olivine, Peridot
Tourmaline, Red: Garnet, Ruby
Turquoise: Chrysocolla

NOTE: Quartz crystals can be charged with the magical attributes of any stone, as can opals, through your visualization.

BIRTHSTONES

I have avoided mentioning these in the text. This is partly because so many other books have listed various stones for each of the signs of the zodiac. Also, there is little agreement as to the "correct" birthstones.

While this isn't an ancient magical tradition, it is well known today, and a book of this type wouldn't be complete without examining them, even briefly. Hence, the following lists.

As with all magical symbolism, these correspondences are suggestions only. They are (generally) based on the planetary ruler(s) of each sign.

If you decide to wear a stone because it is associated with your Sun Sign, remember to do so *only* if you wish to bring that particular stone's influences into your life.

ARIES
Bloodstone
Garnet
Ruby

TAURUS
Emerald
Jade
Lapis Lazuli

GEMINI
Agate
Aventurine

CANCER
Beryl
Moonstone
Sapphire

LEO
Amber
Carnelian
Diamond
Topaz

VIRGO
Agate
Aventurine

LIBRA
Chrysoprase
Lapis Lazuli
Turquoise

SCORPIO
Kunzite
Spinel
Tourmalated Quartz

AQUARIUS
Aquamarine
Fossils
Jet

SAGITTARIUS
Amethyst
Sugilite

PISCES
Amethyst
Sugilite

CAPRICORN
Apache Tear
Hematite
Onyx

Appendix:
Stone Sources

Although we can find stones all around us, many of the more unusual ones can be difficult to obtain.

As I outlined in Chapter Six, stones can be purchased at local rock and lapidary shops. Many natural history museums also sell stone specimens.

Additionally, a number of reliable mail-order sources exist. The most current listing of suppliers willing to sell stones by mail can be found in the latest edition of *Lapidary Journal*. In it are listed dealers who sell staurolite, fossils, cat's-eye, tourmaline and many other stones and minerals. Although not magically oriented, the magazine also contains articles on the folklore and archaeology of stones as well as beautiful full-color photographs. Their address is:

Lapidary Journal
P.O. Box 80937
San Diego, CA 92138

Boji Inc. is the original source for the mysterious objects they named Boji™ stones, and offer the finest quality specimens. They can be contacted at:

Boji Inc.
4682 Shaw Blvd.
Westminster, CO 80030

Isis, also known as Isis Books, is a complete occult supply shop and bookstore in Denver. Their selection of crystals and stones is wide and varied. Among other oddities, Isis stocks the rare Boji stones, which they introduced me to while I was teaching there in May 1987. Write for information regarding catalog price to:

Isis
5701 E. Colfax Ave.
Denver, CO 80220

Charmoon, a friend from northern California, sells crystals, body-work wands, jewelry, tourmalines and an astonishing variety of magical stones. Charmoon also gives crystal parties, workshops and classes. I hope he writes his book soon. He can be contacted at:

Inner Earth
Charmoon Richardson
P.O. Box 1366
Sonoma, CA 95476

Dialing (707) 528-9165 will connect you to his answering machine for questions regarding availability of specific stones.

Uma Silbey, author of the highly successful *The Complete Crystal Guidebook,* offers a fine selection of crystal and stone jewelry and tools. She can be contacted at (415) 453-8845. For a catalog send #2.00 and a SASE (self-addressed, stamped envelope) to:

UMA
P.O. Box 31131
San Francisco, CA 94131

Eye of the Cat is offering a new, complete catalog of supplies (including crystals and stones) that incorporates much magical information. They're happy to receive phone calls at (213) 438-3569. Their catalog is available for $5.00 (nonrefundable) from:

Eye of the Cat
3314 E. Broadway
Long Beach, CA 90803

The Crystal Cave is one of the oldest, most well-established occult and metaphysical supply stores in the greater Los Angeles area. They stock quartz crystal and many unusual stones, including meteorite. Send for a catalog or information to:

The Crystal Cave
415 West Foothill Blvd.
Claremont, CA 91711

Glossary

Akasha: The fifth element, the omnipresent spiritual power that permeates the universe. It is related to outer space, inner space, the unmanifest, and the life force. *See also* ELEMENTS, the.

Amulet: A magically empowered object which deflects energies; a protective object, often worn or carried. *See also* TALISMAN.

Astral Projection: The act of separating the consciousness from the physical body and moving it about at will.

Cabochon: A cut and polished stone, round, oval or square-shaped with one "rough" edge. Cabochons are often used in jewelry.

Charge, to: To magically imbue with power, generally utilizing visualization to direct the power into the object or place.

Chatoyancy: The property, found in many stones, of showing movement, illumination or opalescence within the stone itself. Tiger's-eye, cat's-eye, moonstone, sunstone and many others exhibit this phenomenon.

Deep Consciousness: The PSYCHIC MIND (*see also*).

Divination: The magical art of discovering the unknown by interpreting the random patterns or symbols within clouds, crystal spheres, reflective stones, tarot cards, flames, a PENDULUM (*see also*) and smoke. Divination contacts the PSYCHIC MIND (*see also*) by tricking or drowsing the conscious mind through ritual and observation or manipulation of tools. Those who can easily attain communication with the psychic mind do not need to perform divination, although they may do so.

197

Electrum: The product of blending various metals, such as gold and silver. Rarely found in nature, electrum has a long magical history.

Elements, the: Earth, Air, Fire and Water. These four essences are the building blocks of the universe. Everything that exists (or that has the potential to exist) contains one or more of these energies. The elements are also at large in the world and within ourselves, and can be utilized through magic to cause change. *See also* AKASHA.

Evil Eye: The supposed glance capable of inflicting great harm to others. Also: envy, PSYCHIC ATTACK *(see also)*.

High Priestess: A female practitioner of Wicca who has reached a high status within the religion, passing several tests and receiving (usually) three initiations.

Kahuna: A practitioner of the old Hawaiian philosophical, scientific and magical system; an expert, a magician, a priest or priestess.

Magic: The act of rousing, directing and releasing energy toward a goal. The art of using little-understood but natural powers to cause needed change.

Magician: One who practices magic.

Medicine Bag: *See* POWER BAG.

Meditation: Reflection, contemplation, turning inward. A quiet time in which the practitioner may dwell upon particular thoughts or symbols, or allow them to come unbidden.

Pendulum: A tool of DIVINATION *(see also)* consisting of a string attached to a heavy object, such as a quartz crystal, root, or ring. The free end of the string is held in the hand, the elbow steadied against a flat surface, and a question asked. The movement of the heavy object's swings determines the answer. This is a tool which contacts the PSYCHIC MIND *(see also)*.

Pentagram: A five-pointed star, visualized with one point up, representing the five senses, the ELEMENTS *(see also)*, the hand, the human body. It is a protective symbol known to have been in use since the days of old Babylon. Today it is frequently identified with WICCA *(see also)*.

Power Bag: A SHAMAN'S *(see also)* source of power; a container of cloth, animal skin, and so on in which quartz crystals, stones, drums, rattles and other magical objects are placed.

Projective Energy: That which is electrical, forward-moving, active. Projective energy is protective. *See also* RECEPTIVE ENERGY.

Projective Hand: In right-handed people, the right hand. In left-handers, the left. This is the hand through which magical energy passes from the body. *See also* RECEPTIVE HAND.

Psychic Attack: The supposed direction of negative energy toward another person to harm them; a "hex" or "curse." These are rare today, if not nonexistent.

Psychic Mind: The subconscious, or deep conscious, mind, in which we receive psychic impulses. The psychic mind is at work when we sleep, dream, meditate, employ DIVINATION (*see also*) and experience intuition, or unbidden psychic awareness.

Psychism: The act of being consciously psychic.

Receptive Energy: The opposite of PROJECTIVE ENERGY (*see also*); magnetic, soothing, attracting energy often used for meditation, promoting love, calm and quiet.

Receptive Hand: The left hand in right-handed people; the reverse for left-handed persons. This is the hand through which energy is absorbed into the body. *See also* PROJECTIVE HAND.

Reincarnation: The doctrine of rebirth. The phenomenon of repeated incarnations in human form to allow evolution of the sexless, ageless soul.

Runes: Sticklike letters, remnants of ancient alphabets. These symbols are carved or painted onto stones which are then used to determine possible future trends. They are also used in image magic and have long been thought to possess powers.

Sexual Dysfunction: The inability to engage in, sustain or enjoy shared sexual activities. Impotency and frigidity are two types of dysfunction.

Shaman: A man or woman who has obtained knowledge of other dimensions as well as of the Earth, usually through periods of alternate states of consciousness. This knowledge gives the shaman the power to change this world through magic. Once known derisively as "medicine men" and "witch doctors," shamans are once again respected as repositories of traditional healing, psychological and magical knowledge.

Shamanism: The practice of SHAMANS (*see also*), usually ritualistic or magical in nature, and sometimes religious.

Spell: A magical rite, usually nonreligious in nature and often accompanied by spoken words.

Striations: Fine grooves or lines which are found on certain stones, such as kunzite.

Talisman: An object charged (*see* CHARGE, to) with magical energy to attract a specific force or power to the bearer. *See also* AMULET.

Visualization: The process of forming mental images. In magic, images are formed of the needed magical goal and used to direct energy to cause change.

Wicca: A contemporary Pagan religion with spiritual roots in SHAMANISM (*see also*) and in the earliest expressions of reverence for nature as manifestations of deity. Among its features are the reverence of the universal energy, the ultimate source of all life, as a Goddess and a God.

Witchcraft: Usually folk magic—that is, practical and earthy spells designed to improve the spell-caster's life. Witchcraft and WICCA (*see also*) are often used interchangeably, producing confusion. Many of those who call themselves 'Witch' are not Wiccans but spell-casters or magicians.

Yin/Yang: The twin poles of energy. The yin/yang concept is one system of viewing the universal energies. Yin corresponds to RECEPTIVE ENERGY (*see also*) and yang to PROJECTIVE ENERGY (*see also*).

Annotated Bibliography

In an effort to make this book as complete as possible, I have relied on a number of sources.

I've written down my experiments and experiences with stones; questioned friendly lapidaries, rockhounds, and store owners; grilled my Wiccan and magical friends; and spent many nights and mornings reading through shelves of books and magazines to supplement the firsthand information I was compiling. I try not to take authors at their word. Where possible I have confirmed information found in books with living sources.

The books and magazine articles listed below are a representative sample of those I studied. Anyone wishing to delve more deeply into the mysteries of stone magic can do so by reading these works.

I have appended short comments concerning each source.

Happy reading!

Adams, Evangeline. *Astrology for Everyone.* Philadelphia: Blakiston, 1931.
This work, one of the earliest popular books on astrology of the current age, contains some conflicting but interesting information on birthstones.

Agrippa, Henry Cornelius. *The Philosophy of Natural Magic.* Antwerp, 1531. Reprint. Secaucus, N.J.: University Books, 1974.
Agrippa's classic work contains information on magical uses of stones as well as their planetary correspondences.

"Aima." *Perfumes, Candles, Seals, and Incense.* Los Angeles: Foibles, 1975.

This book contains a fine chapter on the magical uses of precious stones.

Alderman, Clifford Lindsey. *Symbols of Magic: Amulets and Talismans.* New York: Julian Messner, 1977.
Contains interesting information, gleaned from standard sources, regarding stones.

Banis, Victor. *Charms, Spells and Curses for the Millions.* Los Angeles: Sherbourne Press, 1970.
Stone lore from a variety of sources is scattered throughout this book. (I always ignore the "curses.")

Bannerman-Phillips, E. Ivy A. *Amulets and Birthstones: Their Astrological Significance.* Los Angeles: Llewellyn, 1950.
A comprehensive collection of gemstone magic and lore drawn from all ages.

Barrett, Francis. *The Magus, or Celestial Intelligencer.* London, 1801. Reprint. New York: University Books, 1967.
Barrett repeats much of Agrippa's information regarding stones but also includes information relating stones to the elements.

Beckwith, Martha. *Hawaiian Mythology.* Honolulu: University Press of Hawaii, 1940. Reprint. Honolulu: University Press of Hawaii, 1979.
Information regarding the mystic uses and symbolism of stones in ancient Hawaii is included in this exhaustive study.

Best, Michael R., and Frank H. Brightman, eds. *The Book of Secrets of Albertus Magnus of the Virtues of Herbs, Stones and Certain Beasts.* London: Oxford University Press, 1973.
A literate, intelligible translation of the pseudo-Albertus Magnus manuscripts, a collection of which was first published in English around 1550. Magical information regarding stones in this book is somewhat quaint, but useable information can be found, and it's good to think that, if nothing else, it's over four hundred years old.

Bowness, Charles. *The Witch's Gospel.* London: Robert Hale, 1979.
Magical information regarding jet.

Budge, E. A. Wallis. *Amulets and Talismans.* New Hyde Park, N.Y.: University Books, 1968.
Perhaps the classic work regarding magical objects, Budge's book

has had a profound impact on contemporary authors. It is a good survey of ancient stone magic. This work, together with Kunz's and, perhaps Fernie's, contains as much magical stone information as most of the rest of the books listed here put together.

Cirlot, J. E. *A Dictionary of Symbols.* New York: Philosophical Library, 1962.
The symbolism of fossils, meteorites, iron, gold and so on is covered here, with hints at magical applications.

Clifford, Terry. *Cures.* New York: Macmillan, 1980.
This lively look at ancient and modern folk medicine includes a few references to gemstones and crystals.

Coffin, Tristram P., and Hennig Cohen, eds. *Folklore in America.* Garden City, N.Y.: Anchor, 1970.
Iron and ring information.

Crow, W. B. *Precious Stones: Their Occult Power and Hidden Significance.* London: Aquarian Press, 1970.
Some interesting information regarding attribution of stones to the planets and the deities is included.

Daniels, Cora Linn, ed. *Encyclopedia of Superstitions, Folklore and the Occult Sciences of the World.* 3 vols. Detroit: Gale Research Co., 1971.
The chapter named "The Mineral Kingdom" is a fine collection of stone magic and lore.

de Lys, Claudia. *A Treasury of American Superstitions.* New York: Philosophical Library, 1948.
A short chaper entitled "Eyes of the Gods" concerns gemstone magic.

Eichler, Lillian. *The Customs of Mankind.* Garden City, N.Y.: Doubleday, 1924.
Information regarding the magical associations of iron.

Eliade, Mircea. *Images and Symbols: Studies in Religious Symbolism.* New York: Sheed & Ward, 1961.
Myths and ritual uses of coral.

Elkin, A. P. *The Australian Aborigines.* New York: Doubleday, 1964.
Information relating to Aboriginal uses of quartz crystals.

Evans, Joan. *Magical Jewels of the Middle Ages and the Renaissance.* 1922.

Reprint. New York: Dover, 1976.
A scholarly examination of magical lapidaries from ancient times through the 18th century. Interesting, but many passages are in Latin, Greek, and French, even archaic Spanish.

Fernie, William T. *The Occult and Curative Powers of Precious Stones.* 1907. Reprint. New York: Harper & Row, 1973.
Another basic book. Though the information is poorly organized, dozens of stones are thoroughly covered. Much of Fernie's information is culled from medieval and Renaissance manuscripts and so is unavailable elsewhere, except perhaps in Kunz's book.

Fielding, William J. *Strange Superstitions and Magical Practices.* New York: Blakiston, 1943.
Fielding's sensationally titled book contains an excellent chapter concerning gemstone magic and folk rituals.

Frazer, James. *The Golden Bough: A Study in Magic and Religion.* New York: Macmillan, 1956.
Ritual uses of stones are included in this work.

Ghosn, M. T. *Origin of Birthstones and Stone Legends.* Lomita, Calif.: Inglewood Lapidary, 1984.
I picked up this book at a rock show. It's a fine collection of gemstone magic and lore.

Giles, Carl H., and Barbara Ann Williams. *Bewitching Jewelry: Jewelry of the Black Art.* Cranbury, N.J.: A. S. Barnes, 1976.
This curious book contains a chapter concerning occult jewelry, in general, and a short list of gemstones with their magical qualities.

Gleadow, Rupert. *The Origin of the Zodiac.* New York: Atheneum, 1968.
Includes a chapter on astrological birthstones, collating several different systems.

Gregor, Arthur S. *Amulets, Talismans and Fetishes.* New York: Scribner's, 1975.
A book written for "young readers," this work includes much information on the magic of stones used as amulets and talismans.

Hand, Wayland, Anna Cassetta, and Sondra B. Theiderman, eds. *Popular Beliefs and Superstitions: A Compendium of American Folklore.* 3 vols. Boston: G. K. Hall, 1981.

This monumental collection includes many references to folk beliefs, rituals and spells involving gemstones, "rocks" and jewelry.

Harner, Michael. *The Way of the Shaman.* New York: Harper & Row, 1980.
Mr. Harner's introduction to shamanism contains some quartz crystal information.

Harvey, Anne. *Jewels.* New York: Putnam's, 1981.
A charming, beautifully illustrated book relating gemstone legends and lore.

Hayes, Carolyn H. *Pergemin: Perfumes, Incenses, Colors, Birthstones, Their Occult Properties and Uses.* Chicago: Aries Press, 1937.
This pamphlet contains an excellent chapter on the magical uses of stones and, only briefly, addresses birthstones.

Hodges, Doris M. *Healing Stones.* Perry: Pyramid Publishers of Iowa, 1961.
This book contains short chapters on sixteen gemstones, surveying their mythological and magical backgrounds.

Isaacs, Thelma. *Gemstones, Crystals and Healing.* Black Mountain, N.C.: Lorien House, n.d.
A fine book on stone magic, with an emphasis on their healing properties.

Kapoor, Gouri Shanker. *Gems and Astrology: A Guide to Health, Happiness and Prosperity.* New Delhi, India: Ranjan Publications, 1985.
A contemporary survey of ancient and modern Indian gemstone magic, with an emphasis on astrology and healing.

Kenyon, Theda. *Witches Still Live.* New York: Ives Washburn, 1929.
This delightful collection of folklore and magic contains a smattering of stone lore.

Krythe, Maymie. *All About the Months.* New York: Harper & Row, 1966.
This fascinating compendium of calendar lore contains articles concerning birthstones.

Kunz, George Frederick. *The Curious Lore of Precious Stones.* Philadelphia: Lippincott, 1913, 1941. Reprint. New York: Dover, 1977.
Another classic work, Kunz's book is a primary source for students and practitioners of gemstone magic. Its information is drawn from

dozens of ancient books and manuscripts. (Kunzite, by the way, was named in honor of Mr. Kunz.)

Kunz, George Frederick. *Rings for the Finger.* 1917. Reprint. New York: Dover, 1973.
An in-depth investigation of rings throughout history. Two chapters discuss magical and healing rings.

Lame Deer, John [Fire], and Richard Erdoes. *Lame Deer, Seeker of Visions.* New York: Quokka, 1978.
Discussions of the symbolism of pipestone among the Sioux.

Leach, Maria, ed. *Standard Dictionary of Folklore, Mythology and Legend.* New York: Funk & Wagnalls, 1972.
This excellent dictionary contains many articles regarding stone lore and magic.

Leland, Charles Godfrey. *Etruscan Magic and Occult Remedies.* New Hyde Park, N.Y.: University Books, 1963.
Lead divination is discussed in this fascinating work.

Masse, Henri. *Persian Beliefs and Customs.* New Haven: Human Relations Area Files, 1954.
Magic concerning rocks and stones is included in this curiously comprehensive volume.

Maple, Eric. *Superstition: Are You Superstitious?* Cranbury, N.J.: A. S. Barnes, 1972.
A bit of stone magic.

Mella, Dorothee L. *Stone Power: The Legendary and Practical Use of Gems and Stones.* Albuquerque, N. Mex.: Domel, 1976.
One of the earliest books which spurred the current wave of interest in gemstone magic, Mella's work is a fine introduction. A revised edition of this book is now available, as is *Stone Power II.*

Paulsen, Kathryn. *The Complete Book of Magic and Witchcraft.* New York: Signet, 1971.
Another fine compendium of extracts from various ancient writings, this work contains numerous stones and their magical uses.

Pavitt, William. *The Book of Talismans, Amulets and Zodiacal Gems.* 1914. Reprint. No. Hollywood: Wilshire, 1970.
(Though "William Pavitt" is given as the author's name on the spine and front cover of this book, the actual authors seem to be William

Thomas and Kate Pavitt.) This book contains a good section on gemstones.

Pearl, Richard M. *How to Know the Minerals and Rocks.* New York: McGraw-Hill, 1955.
A nonmagical work describing 125 gems, minerals and rocks.

Pliny the Elder [Caius Plinius Secundus]. *Natural History.* Cambridge: Harvard University Press, 1956.
This monumental work culls much of the stone magic that was in use in Rome around the first century C.E. It is heavily quoted in other books. Although Pliny was a skeptic, he duly recorded many of the old magical beliefs.

Randolph, Vance. *Ozark Superstitions.* New York: Cambridge University Press, 1947.
Ring and jewelry beliefs of the peoples living in the Ozarks.

Raphael, Katrina. *Crystal Enlightenment: The Transforming Properties of Crystals and Healing Stones Vol. 1.* New York: Aurora Press, 1985.
One of the "new" books on stone healing, this work contains much information that is workable and coherent. Some of it is 'channelled'.

Raphael, Katrina. *Crystal Healing: The Therapeutic Application of Crystals and Stones Vol. 2.* New York: Aurora Press, 1987.
More of the same, again 'channelled'. Interesting reading but much of it seems a bit far-fetched to me. A portion of this book is involved with some fascinating methods of laying stones directly on the body to activate the chakras. (By the way, you can safely ignore the references to volumes in the title. There is no volume one of this book, nor a volume two of the above.)

Richardson, Wally, Jenny Richardson, and Lenora Huett. *Spiritual Value of Gemstones.* Marina del Rey, Calif.: Devorss, 1980.
This work, another 'channelled' book, contains some excellent information regarding stones, although marred by unintentional sexist terminology.

Schmidt, Phillip. *Superstition and Magic.* Westminster, Md.: Newman Press, 1963.
This book, written by a Jesuit, contains some excellent information on gemstone magic, if you overlook the author's obvious distaste for the subject.

"Seleneicthon." *Applied Magic.* Hialeah, Fla.: Mi-World, n.d.
Planetary attributions of stones.

Shah, Sayed Idries. *The Secret Lore of Magic.* New York: Citadel, 1970.
Planetary information relating to gemstones is contained in this collection of ancient magical *grimoires.*

Sharon, Douglas. *Wizard of the Four Winds: A Shaman's Story.* New York: Free Press, 1978.
Uses of quartz crystals and shaped stones among contemporary Peruvian shamans.

Silbey, Uma. *The Complete Crystal Guidebook.* New York: Bantam Books, 1987.
One of the best works on quartz crystal work ever published. Direct, complete, useable information is presented, unhindered by "mystic revelations" and quasi-historical information regarding Atlantis, etc. Many exercises and rituals guide the reader into discovering the powers of crystals. A must book!

Simpson, Jacqueline. *Folklore of Sussex.* London: B. T. Batsford, 1973.
Holey stones are discussed in this work.

Smith, Michael G. *Crystal Power.* St. Paul, Minn.: Llewellyn Publications, 1984.
A variety of applications of quartz crystals are included in this interesting book.

Stein, Diane. *The Women's Spirituality Book.* St. Paul, Minn.: Llewellyn Publications, 1987.
A chapter on quartz crystals and other stones is an excellent introduction to stone magic.

Thomson, H. A. *Legends of Gems: Strange Beliefs Which the Astrological Birthstones Have Collected Through the Ages.* Los Angeles: Graphic Press, 1937.
An interesting early compilation of traditional stone magic, with an emphasis on birthstones.

Thompson, C. J. S. *The Mysteries and Secrets of Magic.* New York: Olympia Press, 1972.
This book contains chapters entitled "Magical Rings" and "Magic in Jewels," both filled with excellent, ancient information.

Toor, Frances. *A Treasury of Mexican Folkways.* New York: Crown, 1973.
A short section discusses Mexican shamans' use of quartz crystals.

Underhill, Ruth. *The Papago Indians of Arizona.* A publication of the Branch of Education, Bureau of Indian Affairs, Department of the Interior. N.d.
This pamphlet, probably printed in the 1940's, contains Papago shamans' use of quartz crystals.

Uyldert, Mellie. *The Magic of Precious Stones.* Wellingborough, England: Turnstone Press, 1981.
A fair collection of gemstone lore and magic. Considering that this work has been translated from Dutch, it is surprisingly easy to read, though perhaps not to understand.

Verrill, A. Hyatt. *Minerals, Metals and Gems.* New York: Grossett & Dunlap, 1939.
A nonmagical introduction to the mineral world.

Villiers, Elizabeth. *The Book of Charms.* London, 1927. Reprint. New York: Simon & Schuster, 1973.
In this modern, revised edition, the chapter entitled "Stones, Jewels and Beads" contains a fine sampling of magical information.

Walker, Barbara. *The Woman's Encyclopedia of Myths and Mysteries.* New York: Harper & Row, 1983.
Stones and metals related to the deities and the planets.

Wright, Elbee. *Book of Legendary Spells.* Minneapolis, Minn.: Marlar Publishing, 1974.
This book contains an alphabetical listing of gemstones and their magical properties.

PUBLICATIONS CONSULTED

Archaeology
A Pagan Renaissance
Circle Network News
Lapidary Journal
National Geographic
The Los Angeles Times
The San Diego Union

INDEX

The page number(s) of the main entry about each stone and metal is *italicized* when there's more than one page reference.

STAY IN TOUCH

On the following pages you will find listed, with their current prices, some of the books now available on related subjects. Your book dealer stocks most of these and will stock new titles in the Llewellyn series as they become available. We urge your patronage.

To obtain our full catalog, to keep informed about new titles as they are released and to benefit from informative articles and helpful news, you are invited to write for our bimonthly news magazine/catalog, *Llewellyn's New Worlds of Mind and Spirit*. A sample copy is free, and it will continue coming to you at no cost as long as you are an active mail customer. Or you may subscribe for just $10.00 in the U.S.A. and Canada ($20.00 overseas, first class mail). Many bookstores also have *New Worlds* available to their customers. Ask for it.

Stay in touch! In *New Worlds'* pages you will find news and features about new books, tapes and services, announcements of meetings and seminars, articles helpful to our readers, news of authors, products and services, special money-making opportunities, and much more.

Llewellyn's New Worlds of Mind and Spirit
P.O. Box 64383-126, St. Paul, MN 55164-0383, U.S.A.
* * *

TO ORDER BOOKS AND TAPES

If your book dealer does not have the books described on the following pages readily available, you may order them directly from the publisher by sending full price in U.S. funds, plus $3.00 for postage and handling for orders *under* $10.00; $4.00 for orders *over* $10.00. There are no postage and handling charges for orders over $50.00. Postage and handling rates are subject to change. UPS Delivery: We ship UPS whenever possible. Delivery guaranteed. Provide your street address as UPS does not deliver to P.O. Boxes. UPS to Canada requires a $50.00 minimum order. Allow 4-6 weeks for delivery. Orders outside the U.S.A. and Canada: Airmail—add retail price of book; add $5.00 for each non-book item (tapes, etc.); add $1.00 per item for surface mail.

FOR GROUP STUDY AND PURCHASE

Because there is a great deal of interest in group discussion and study of the subject matter of this book, we feel that we should encourage the adoption and use of this particular book by such groups by offering a special quantity price to group leaders or agents.

Our special quantity price for a minimum order of five copies of *Cunningham's Encyclopedia of Crystal, Gem & Metal Magic* is $38.85 cash-with-order. This price includes postage and handling within the United States. Minnesota residents must add 6.5% sales tax. For additional quantities, please order in multiples of five. For Canadian and foreign orders, add postage and handling charges as above. Credit card (VISA, MasterCard, American Express) orders are accepted. Charge card orders only ($15.00 minimum order) may be phoned in free within the U.S.A. or Canada by dialing 1-800-THE-MOON. For customer service, call 1-612-291-1970. Mail orders to:

LLEWELLYN PUBLICATIONS
P.O. Box 64383-126, St. Paul, MN 55164-0383, U.S.A.

Prices subject to change without notice.

CRYSTAL POWER
by Michael G. Smith
This is an amazing book, for what it claims to present—with complete instructions and diagrams so that YOU can work them yourself—is the master technology of ancient Atlantis: psionic (mind-controlled and life-energized machines) devices made from common quartz crystals!

These crystal devices seem to work only with the disciplined mind power of a human operator, yet their very construction seems to start a process of growth and development, a new evolutionary step in the human psyche that bridges mind and matter.

Does this "re-discovery" mean that we are living, now, in the New Atlantis? Have these Power Tools been re-invented to meet the needs of this prophetic time? Are Psionic Machines the culminating Power To the People to free us from economic dependence on fossil fuels and smokestack industry? This book answers "yes" to all these questions, and asks you to simply build these devices and put them to work to help bring it all about.
0-87542-725-1, 288 pgs., illus., 5¼ x 8, softcover   **$9.95**

CRYSTAL AWARENESS
by Catherine Bowman
For millions of years, crystals have been waiting for people to discover their wonderful powers. Today they are used in watches, computer chips and communication devices. But there is also a spiritual, holistic aspect to crystals.

Crystal Awareness will teach you everything you need to know about crystals. It will also help those who have been working with them to complete their knowledge. Topics include:, Crystal Forms, Colored and Colorless Crystals, Single Points, Clusters and Double Terminated Crystals, Crystal and Human Energy Fields, The Etheric and Spiritual Bodies, Crystals as Energy Generators, Crystal Cleansing and Programming, Crystal Meditation, The Value of Polished Crystals, Crystals and Personal Spiritual Growth, Crystals and Chakras, How to Make Crystal Jewelry, The Uses for Crystals in the Future, Color Healing, Programming Crystals with Color, Compatible Crystals and Metals, Several Crystal Healing Techniques, including The Star of David Healing.

Crystal Awareness is destined to be the guide of choice for people who are beginning their investigation of crystals.
0-87542-058-3, 200 pgs., Mass Market Format, illus.,   **$3.95**

CRYSTAL SPIRIT
by Michael G. Smith
Crystal Spirit is the book thousands of people have asked for after reading the popular *Crystal Power* by the same author.

Crystal Spirit contains timely and hard-to-find information on:
  • New types of crystal rods
  • Crystal pyramid devices
  • The crystal pipe from Native American traditions
  • Ki and Chi energy through crystals for martial artists
  • Health and exercise with crystal wristbands

The book begins with explanations of crystals of the ancient past and how to reconstruct your own: the Trident Krystallos, Atlantean Crystal Cross, Crux Crystallum. The book ends with a discussion of the new crystal pipe based on traditional Native American practices and the science of Universal Energy. Between these two chapters is a wealth of information and instruction on other crystal inventions, all inexpensive and simple to construct and use, and beneficial for earth healing.
0-87542-726-X, 208 pgs., mass market, illustrated   **$3.95**

THE WOMEN'S BOOK OF HEALING
by Diane Stein

At the front of the women's spirituality movement with her previous books, Diane Stein now helps women (and men) reclaim their natural right to be healers. Included are exercises which can help YOU to become a healer! Learn about the uses of color, vibration, crystals and gems for healing. Learn about the auric energy field and the Chakras.

The book teaches alternative healing theory and techniques and combines them with crystal and gemstone healing, laying on of stones, psychic healing, laying on of hands, chakra work and aura work, color therapy. It teaches beginning theory in the aura, chakras, colors, creative visualization, meditation, health theory and ethics with some quantum theory. 46 gemstones plus clear quartz crystals are discussed in detail, arranged by chakras and colors.

The Women's Book of Healing is a book designed to teach basic healing (Part I) and healing with crystals and gemstones (Part II). Part I discusses the aura and four bodies; the chakras; basic healing skills of creative visualization, meditation and color work; psychic healing; and laying on of hands. Part II begins with a chapter on clear quartz crystal, then enters gemstone work with introductory gemstone material. The remainder of the book discusses, in chakra by chakra format, specific gemstones for healing work, their properties and uses.

0-87542-759-6, 336 pgs., 6 x 9, color plates, softcover **$12.95**

CUNNINGHAM'S ENCYCLOPEDIA OF MAGICAL HERBS
by Scott Cunningham

This is an expansion on the material presented in his first Llewellyn book, *Magical Herbalism*. This is not just another herbal for medicinal uses of herbs—*this is the most comprehensive source of herbal data for magical uses ever printed!* Almost every one of the over 400 herbs are illustrated, making this a great source for herb identification. For each herb you will also find: magical properties, palnetary rulerships, genders, associated deities, folk and Latin names and much more. to make this book even easier to use you will also find a folk name cross reference, and all of the herbs are fully indexed. There is also a large annotated bibliography, and a list of mail order suppliers so you can find the books and herbs you need.

Like all of Scott's books, this one does not require you to use complicated rituals or expensive magical paraphernalia. Instead, it shares with you the *intrinsic* powers of the herbs. Thus, you will be able to discover which herbs, by their very nature, can be used for luck, love, success, money, divination, astral projection, safety, psychic self-defense and much more. Besides being interesting and educational it is also fun, and fully illustrated with unusual woodcuts from old herbals. This book has rapidly become the classic in its field. It enhances books such as 777 and is a must for all Wiccans.

0-87542-122-9, 352 pgs., 6 x 9, illus., softcover **$12.95**

THE MAGICAL HOUSEHOLD
by Scott Cunningham and David Harrington
Whether your home is a small apartment or a palatial mansion, you want it to be something special. Now it can be with *The Maglcal Household*. Learn how to make your home more than just a place to live. Turn it into a place of security, life, fun and magic. Here you will not find the complex magic of the ceremonial magician. Rather, you will learn simple, quick and effective magical spells 'that use nothing more than common items in your house: furniture, windows, doors, carpet, pets, etc. You will learn to take advantage of the intrinsic power and energy that is already in your home, waiting to be tapped. You will learn to make magic a part of your life. The result is a home that is safeguarded from harm and a place which will bring you happiness, health and more.
0-87542-124-5, 208 pgs., 5-1/4 x 8, illus., softcover $8.95

MAGICAL HERBALISM: The Secret Craft of the Wise
by Scott Cunningham
In *Magical Herbalism*, certain plants are prized for the special range of energies—the vibrations, or powers—they possess. Magical Herbalism unites the powers of plants and man to produce, and direct, change in accord with human will and desire.

This is the Magic of amulets and charms, sachets and herbal pillows, incenses and scented oils, simples and infusions and anointments. It's Magic as old as our knowledge of plants, an art that anyone can learn and practice, and once again enjoy as we look to the Earth to rediscover our roots and make inner connections with the world of Nature.

This is Magic that is beautiful and natural—a Craft of Hand and Mind merged with the Power and Glory of Nature: a special kind that does not use the medicinal powers of herbs, but rather the subtle vibrations and scents that touch the psychic centers and stir the astral field in which we live to work at the causal level behind the material world.

This is the Magic of Enchantment . . . of word and gesture to shape the images of mind and channel the energies of the herbs. It is a Magic for *everyone*—for the herbs are easily and readily obtained, the tools are familiar or easily made, and the technology that of home and garden. This book includes step-by-step guidance to the preparation of herbs and to their compounding in incense and oils, sachets and amulets, simples and infusions, with simple rituals and spells for every purpose.
0-87542-120-2, 256 pgs., 5-1/4 x 8, illus., softcover $7.95

EARTH POWER:
TECHNIQUES OF NATURAL MAGIC
by Scott Cunningham

Magick is the art of working with the forces of Nature to bring about necessary, and desired, changes. The forces of Nature—expressed through Earth, Air, Fire and Water—are our "spiritual ancestors" who paved the way for our emergence from the pre-historic seas of creation. Attuning to, and working with these energies in magick not only lends you the power to affect changes in your life, it also allows you to sense your own place in the larger scheme of Nature. Using the "Old Ways" enables you to live a better life, and to deepen your understanding of the world about you. The tools and powers of magick are around you, waiting to be grasped and utilized. This book gives you the means to put Magick into your life, shows you how to make and use the tools, and gives you spells for every purpose.

0-87542-121-0, 176 pgs., 51/4 x 8, illus., softcover   **$8.95**

THE COMPLETE BOOK OF INCENSE, OILS AND BREWS
by Scott Cunningham

For centuries the composition of incenses, the blending of oils, and the mixing of herbs have been used by people to create positive changes in their lives. With this book, the curtains of secrecy have been drawn back, providing you with practical, easy-to-understand information that will allow you to practice these methods of magical cookery.

Scott Cunningham, world-famous expert on magical herbalism, first published *The Magic of Incense, Oils and Brews* in 1986. *The Complete Book of Incense, Oils and Brews* is a revised and expanded version of that book. Scott took readers' suggestions from the first edition and added more than 100 new formulas. Every page has been clarified and rewritten, and new chapters have been added.

There is no special, costly equipment to buy, and ingredients are usually easy to find. The book includes detailed information on a wide variety of herbs, sources for purchasing ingredients, substitutions for hard-to-find herbs, a glossary, and a chapter on creating your own magical recipes.

0-87542-128-8, 288 pgs., 6 x 9, illus., softcover   **$12.95**

CRYSTAL HEALING: The Next Step
by Phyllis Galde

Discover the further secrets of quartz crystal! Now modern research and use have shown that crystals have even more healing and therapeutic properties than have been realized. Learn why polished, smoothed crystal is better to use to heighten your intuition, improve creativity and for healing.

Learn to use crystals for reprogramming your subconscious to eliminate problems and negative attitudes that prevent success. Here are techniques that people have successfully used, not just theories.

This book reveals newly discovered abilities of crystal now accessible to all, and is a sensible approach to crystal use. *Crystal Healing* will be your guide to improve the quality of your life and expand your consciousness.

0-87542-246-2, 224 pgs., mass market, illus.   **$3.95**

Prices subject to change without notice.